SPIRITS ENTWINED

Wojtek K Krajewski

A spiritual autobiography of
International Spiritualist Mediums
Clive N Daniels and Wojtek K Krajewski

Fantine Press

First published in 2008 by

FANTINE PRESS
The Coach House
Stansted Hall
Stansted
Essex CM24 8UD

ISBN 978 1 901958 18 8

Printed in England by Booksprint

This book is dedicated to Clive who has been my inspiration and rock for over 30 years. Without his continuing guidance, support and encouragement I would not have succeeded in reaching many of my goals both spiritual and material. My life has been the richer because of him.

PREFACE

Over the many years that we have both been working and serving spirit we have met and talked to many people all over the UK and abroad. They have shown a great interest in our story and the various incidents that have occurred on our journey which have shaped our lives and at the same time impacted theirs. As a result we have been asked, on numerous occasions, to write all these down in a book. Also on the rare occasions when we have sat in a congregation at the spiritualist churches I have been told, by many mediums, that I should write a book.

After years of dithering I have finally put pen to paper or more correctly fingers to keyboard and here is the result. I do hope that you find it not only interesting but also helpful.

Wojtek

CONTENTS

INTRODUCTION

This book is a true story which currently spans over 70 years. It is of two people whose lives were already spiritually entwined before their respective physical births and subsequently became physically linked years later. They shared a common understanding and purpose in life. It is a story of coming to terms with ones self and what life has dealt you. Of learning and tolerance and having the courage to set yourself free from your own prejudices and accepting the consequences good or bad.

It is to a large extent an autobiography of Mediums Clive Daniels and Wojtek Krajewski and takes us from separate childhood days in Liverpool and London to the first and life changing meeting in Rayners Lane, Middlesex. From there to the many experiences that shaped their spiritual lives as they served spirit in numerous churches, halls and homes around the UK as well as overseas.

It will be of interest to those who are seeking for answers about life and what is termed death as well as the very different routes we as individuals take, only to find out in hindsight that the freewill we thought we had, was in effect already pre-ordained.

Although with humour it is at times a very sad and emotional journey but throughout it remains and is a story of love, learning and acceptance. It will perhaps be of special interest to those who are drawn towards Spiritualism and who may also have seen or know of their public work.

1

CLIVE N. DANIELS

The Beginning

The date is 20th December 1935 at a Nursing Home in Waterloo near Liverpool which is opposite the well known landmark of "Five Lamps". Bertha Daniels (nee Palmer), who is expecting, is admitted into hospital 7 months into her pregnancy with labour pains. After a difficult and long labour a baby boy is born. This is the child who we now know as Clive Noel Daniels. However and surprisingly the labour was not over as further contractions started and some time later another baby boy was born. This child lives only a matter of minutes and passes away. In those days ultra scans were unavailable and pre-natal clinics were not so sophisticated and could not accurately predict if a pregnancy was that of twins.

As a result of the difficult, complicated and long labour, Bertha Daniels also passed away a short time later leaving only one surviving twin. Clive's father Jim could not cope with Clive as he already had three young children (Freda 7, Eric 5, and George 4) so he decided to leave Clive in the Alder Hey Children's Home where he feels he would be better cared for than he could manage.

The months roll by and Clive now is a toddler of some 18 months and still at Alder Hey. His future remains uncertain but a couple from Scotland who visited the home, with a view to adoption and were in the tea business, had seen and fallen in love with this little boy and expressed a keen interest in adopting him. They asked the Children's Home to contact Clive's father and ask if he would be willing to allow the adoption. This was flatly refused but we do not know the reasons why. It could have been because Jim Daniels was a very proud man and fiercely independent and while he had much difficulty coping with his existing children he also refused help from the other members of the family. Similarly adoption to him perhaps meant failure.

In the meantime Clive's father Jim had been courting a woman called Elsa. They first met when Elsa knocked on his front door, as a promotions girl, trying to sell some new bread called Nimble. It was her brief to sign up as many people as possible for a regular weekly delivery. They got talking and Jim invited her in for lunch. This consisted of beans on toast, which was a little delicacy that Elsa had not experienced before. A week later Jim asked Elsa to marry him and she agreed. Elsa was at this time totally unaware that within the family there was another child in addition to the three she knew about. When Jim eventually told her, after they were married, that he had another son, she immediately went to the Children's Home to see this other child called Clive.

As fate had it a few days earlier Clive had received a bang, to the side of his face, due to a fall in his cot and as a result he was very bruised. When Elsa saw the state that Clive was in she created hell with the staff and announced "I am taking him home!" With that announcement she sent out for some clothes. These arrived and comprised, as Clive can still recall, of a white corduroy suite with leggings. She dressed him and then thrust him under her arm and stormed out of the hospital. Indeed one of Clive's earliest memories is being carried out horizontally from the hospital by some strange woman he had never seen before.

Clive's childhood was one of great solitude and emptiness. Here was a child who craved affection but never once did his father or stepmother ever hug or cuddle him, no bedtime kiss, no touch, just nothing throughout his childhood. Indeed he did not know that his mother was in fact a stepmother until he was 14 years old. This lack of emotional fulfilment may have been instrumental in developing Clive's affection and bonding to animals which he could hold, hug, stroke and love. His father Jim was a strange man who to the outside world was a "lovely and kind man, a perfect gentleman" but to his family and particularly his children he was feared terribly. While he had on occasions beaten his brothers and sister with a leather belt and one time even used a horse whip, he never struck Clive. But Clive nonetheless was terrified of him. There were occasions where his father just had to give Clive a severe look and Clive would wet himself with fear.

He had a very cruel streak within him that he displayed to Clive on far too many occasions. There are many examples of this and a few are highlighted here to give you an idea of the torture and anguish that was tearing this young child apart.

Clive's father owned and ran a Boarding Kennel business where he also bred dogs so that he could sell the puppies. When Clive was about 6 years old his father came home one day and totally unexpected, presented Clive with a puppy dog which he gave to him as his own to look after. Clive was thrilled to have this little puppy that he could look after and love. He named him "Lucky" and developed a very strong bond with this dog who would always wait patiently but anxiously for Clive to come back from school. The two of them were inseparable.

One day Clive as usual rushed back from school, looking forward to being greeted by an excited Lucky, but his dog was not at home. He searched everywhere getting more and more concerned. Then a distraught Clive rushed over to his father and asked "daddy where is my dog?" His father said bluntly and without any emotion or concern "I sold him!" Clive was deeply shocked and devastated. Can any of us truly imagine the distress and mental cruelty such an action made on this sensitive child.

On another occasion some time later he was given a black and white collie from the kennels in Waterloo. Again this was unexpected and Clive again bonded with this dog. After looking after him for some time his father, without any explanation, instructed him to take the dog to the vet and have him put down and "wait for the lead!" Clive who was now almost hysterical, pleaded with his father but all to no avail. So he took the dog to the vet and had to watch his beloved dog being placed into a gas chamber and remembers hearing the dog's whimpering and squeaking as it was overcome with the gas fumes as it took its final breaths. He brought the lead home as instructed.

Time and life moved on again. Now Clive had a very good singing voice and would often sing standing in the back of a lorry which was parked up on the Pier Head at Liverpool. One day following a singing competition at Lineaker Mission he won a prize which was a Postal Order. When asked by his father what he was going to spend the money on. A very excited Clive said "it would be on a new dog and some galoshes!" He bought both the galoshes and a brown and white terrier puppy that he named "Lassie". Again the months pass and Lassie grows. Clive is told by his father to "push the dog out" so that it can get some exercise as Clive was not allowed to walk it alone. One day the dog went missing, when it came in season, but did return a few days later. Unbeknown to Clive she had been mated. Lassie just grew and got fat as far as Clive was concerned because he did not know or understand what had happened to her. He was then told by his father, for no reason that Clive could understand, not to let her into the house but leave her outside and totally ignore her. Even when he went to school and she would follow, he was not allowed to acknowledge her. Lassie would sit all day at the school gates and again follow Clive home but he again had to ignore her as he was so frightened of his father. He longed to hold and stroke her and could see the puzzled look in the dogs eyes as she could not understand Clive's changed behaviour towards her. This was all tearing him apart but the penalty for disobedience would be catastrophic. Soon after Lassie just disappeared and was not seen again. Clive was 11 years old.

Clive like most young boys did have a mischievous side which he did on occasion utilise. One such situation did involve the dogs at his father's kennels or perhaps more correctly "the residue" that the dogs left behind in large lumps of waste that they had excreted. In those days the disposal of such waste from a kennels was quite a considerable problem which required some "inspired thinking" to solve.

Clive's father pondered this problem for a while and came upon a solution. He instructed Clive to go to the local shoe shop and bring back as many shoe boxes as he could carry. This Clive did and then his father very carefully filled a shoe box with the dog "residue" replaced the lid and then wrapped the box in crisp brown paper and completing the parcel by tying it all together with fresh white string, ensuring two finger loops for carrying were provided. He then gave the parcel to Clive and asked him to dispose of it.

Clive attached the parcel to his bike and cycled to Woolworths in Waterloo. There he took it into the shop and went over to the jewellery counter where he discreetly left it on the floor and then retired to a good observation point and waited.

Some minutes later two people approached the counter to look at the jewellery. They were a middle aged couple dressed rather smartly, he in a suit and she in a dress suit. As they browsed the counter the lady suddenly noticed the unattended parcel on the floor. She nudged her husband and secretively pointed to the floor. He looked down and acknowledged her "find". They both tried to keep a normal demeanour while whispering to each other how they could retrieve the parcel without raising any suspicion. They shuffled towards the parcel. A few moments passed and then the man looked up and down the aisles of the store and very casually bent down and picked up the parcel. They both then quickly scurried out the store at quite a pace looking very pleased with their trophy dangling beside them.

One can only imagine the situation when they got home and opened the parcel with eager anticipation only to be confronted with a pile of stinking dog s**t. Clive repeated this disposal technique many times much to his amusement, and no doubt the recipients fury.

Since early childhood Clive had problems with his ears and as a baby had a mastoid operation to one ear. When he was about thirteen he had his other ear operated on for the same condition. After the procedure Clive was very self-conscious of the way he looked because the hospital had to shave off all of his hair on one side of his head. As a result he would not go out but just stayed home.

However his father got fed up with Clive being at home all the time so told him to go out. This Clive reluctantly did and as expected he got some peculiar looks from people as he walked down the street. Keen to avoid any more embarrassment Clive went into a Salvation Army hall where he felt he would be safe. A service was being held and the band were playing and accompanied with the usual joyful singing by the full congregation.

Clive sat down at the back of the hall and started to relax a bit and just take in the atmosphere. After about 15 minutes a smiling Salvation Army officer came up to Clive and whispered in his ear. Unfortunately he whispered in the ear that Clive had had the operation so his hearing was still very poor. Clive thought the officer said "Would you like a cup of tea?" As he was thirsty he said "Oh yes please" to which the officer replied "Good. Follow me."

He led Clive down to the front of the full church and told him to kneel down at the alter. Clive thought to himself that this was rather a strange way to get a cup of tea but nonetheless complied with the instruction. Then the minister came forward and started to recite "The Pledge" and on completion asked Clive to sign it and so become a member of the Salvation Army.

It later transpired that what the officer actually said to Clive earlier was "Would you like to come to Jesus?"

Spiritual Awakening

It was in his childhood that Clive first started to experience what we would now call paranormal activities. When he was about 4 years old he would often see a lady standing at the end of his bed with a baby in her arms, just before he was going to sleep. He was puzzled by this lady. Who was she and why did she come? But it did not frighten him. When Clive was 14 he was being shown photographs in an album by his grandmother. It was there that he saw a photo of this same lady that he would see at bedtime. He asked who she was and was told that it was his mother. But in his mind this could not be so, because he already had a mother (Elsa). It then had to be explained to him that Elsa was in fact his stepmother and that his birth mother died when he was still a baby.

Clive began to "see" more and more of these spirit people and assumed that, like him, everyone else could also see them. But he soon learnt that this was not the case. During the war years of 1939-45 when a young Clive would go shopping with his stepmother, he would often "see" the spirit forms (these were the spirit forms of those who had been killed in action) of soldiers in uniform standing beside people in the shops. He would say in a voice which was always too loud "mummy who is that man standing by the lady?" His mother would snap back at him "stop it and don't be so silly!" So after a while, although Clive continued to see spirit, he just stopped mentioning it because he knew he would be scolded.

Often on a Saturday or Sunday his stepmother would lay out a great tea that consisted of a great feast of cakes and sweets. When Clive would see the table full of all these good things it literally took his breath away and several times he "apparently fainted" and started mumbling in a completely incoherent manner. Doctor Novak the family GP would be called out and after an examination would say that there is nothing to worry about and that Clive would grow out of it. This we now know was the beginnings of his association with his key Spirit Guide and his trance work. More on this later.

Clive's life continued to be unhappy at this time and he also still continued to see spirit. This angered his father greatly who thought that Clive was going mad with some severe mental and delusional problems. He had by now had enough and decided that it was time to have Clive sectioned under the then current mental health provisions and put into a mental institution. Arrangements had already been made by him and a place found in an institution some miles away from Lancaster. So on one particular evening he told Clive to go to Lime Street station in Liverpool and check the times of the trains that would take them to Lancaster station. There a car would meet them, as there was no public transport and take them to the institution. He did not tell Clive the real reason for the trip but instead told him that it was to do with a job for him. Clive had no idea that this was his father's plan for his future.

So at 14 years of age Clive arrives at Lime Street station to ask for the train times. He approached the ticket kiosk and the man inside looked up and said "Yes". Why Clive responded in the way he did he does not know but he said hesitantly "London please". "Single or return?" asked the man. "Single" replied Clive and with that he purchased a ticket and sat waiting on the platform. Later that evening, he caught the midnight train to London. The journey was long and thankfully uneventful. He could not sleep on the train because he was frightened and also nervous of some of the other passengers.

London (and back)

At about 6.00am he arrived at Euston Station in London, just in the clothes he stood, with half a crown (equivalent to 12.5p) in his pocket, no friends and nowhere to go. He was tired, hungry and very alone. The year was 1950.

Clive just started walking, he had no idea where he was heading but walked and walked. After several hours he saw a notice in a shop window advertising for an assistant. The shop was Barnum's Theatrical Costumers in Olympia just opposite the exhibition centre. He went in and applied for the job. After a short interview he was offered the job there and then with an immediate start. Trouble was that he would not get paid for a fortnight so he now had to manage without money and so no food until then.

After the shop closed, on his first day, he was in effect on the street with nowhere to stay. He wandered around and noticed a children's school close by. It was locked and deserted so he scrambled over the gate and made his way to the outside toilet block. This would now be his home till he could afford something better.

That same evening as he walked the streets the hunger pains increased. He saw a lady with a push chair with a young child eating an apple. The child threw the apple away and when they had passed by, Clive picked up the apple and ate what was left of it.

Shortly after that he met and got talking to a young lad who, after a little while, invited Clive for a coffee and bun at the "Black & White Coffee House". The lad paid at the till by taking his money from the safety of his sock. Clive asked how did he get his money and the lad explained that he worked at Lyons Corner House in Piccadilly. There he worked through the night washing and cleaning. He told Clive that if he wanted he could come with him and he would see if he could get him in as a "causal".

They arrived at Lyons late into the evening and Clive had to queue along with the other casual hopefuls. The lad put in a good word for Clive and he was picked for the night shift. He worked hard most of the night and was able to eat any food that had been left over. He ate well that night. In the morning he was back working in the shop. This same procedure went on for a couple of weeks and fortunately Clive was picked every night.

After a few weeks of struggling Clive had accumulated some money and started his search for more suitable accommodation. He looked through the papers and found out that he could afford to rent a bed-sit in Kilburn. It was a three story house, his little room was on the top floor and he was the only white resident. The others were all black and female. He was fearful and therefore kept his door locked at all times.

At this house there were always many "comings and goings" of strangers which could be day or night. After a while Clive realised that this was because the ladies in the house were "working girls" and brought their clients back. However these very same girls showed Clive extreme kindness and always checked on a regular basis that he was alright and had enough to eat. A few months later Clive had saved some more money and was able to afford a better bed-sit and so moved to Barnes.

It was while in Barnes that he started to look for another job and shortly afterward he was employed at a dry cleaning shop, in the quadrant at Richmond. There he was responsible for processing all the different garments and dealing with customers.

Months passed by and Clive eventually decided it was time to return back to Liverpool. Since he had run away he had not made any contact with his family nor had his father tried to find him or even report him missing to the Police.

When Clive returned home and rang the bell of the house he was not greeted with any warmth, affection or anger. Just total indifference. So he quickly decided that the best thing to do was to try and get a job and be away from home. He looked through the local papers and found an advert for a waiter at the North Wales & Cheshire Gliding Club in Eastham, on the Wirral. He applied for the position and was asked to come for an interview. The interview was with a Mrs. Belcher who was joint owner. It went well and as a result he was offered the position. He would be paid thirty shillings a week (£1.50) plus any tips. His week would commence on a Tuesday through to the following Sunday. Monday was his day off. It was a live-in position.

Clive was very successful in this position and worked hard and diligently. As a result he was popular with the clientele who would often ask if he could wait on their table. One special and memorable client was a Director at Cammell Laird the local shipbuilders. He and his guests would always come on a Friday afternoon, just at the end of service which should have finished at two o'clock. Because of this the waiters were not keen to serve and if they did their attitude was not of the best. Clive being keen did not mind and served with his usual efficiency and enthusiasm.

After the meal was completed, well after 4 o'clock, the bill would be paid. He would then be called over to the table and the host would say to Clive (who he nicknamed daffodil on account of Clive's very slim figure) "this is just for you". With that he placed a very neatly folded and crisp piece of paper into Clive's hand. In the staff-room Clive opened his hand and unfolded the paper. It was a brand new white five pound note. This tip was given to Clive each and every time and lasted many months.

It was a good job to because Clive's father always demanded his wages of 30 shillings, in full, when he visited home each Monday on his day off. It was also good that his father had no idea how much Clive got in tips as, no doubt, most of that would have had to be relinquished too.

Clive really enjoyed his work at the Gliding Club. Weekends were, naturally, always busy. Particularly so when wedding receptions were held. However when Clive visited home one day on his day off he was instructed by his father that he would have to be present at home the following Saturday so that they could visit his maternal aunt. Someone who Clive had never met before and lived in Bentham, Yorkshire. Clive explained that he could not come as he was already committed at the Gliding Club with a long standing wedding reception. His father dismissed this with a wave of the hand and told Clive to tell his employer that he needed the time off and that was the end of the matter.

When Clive returned to the Gliding Club he explained

the position to the owner Mrs Belcher. She told him that he could not be spared as not only was he a vital staff member, there was also nobody else who could take his place. Clive relayed this information to his father but all to no avail as he reiterated to Clive that he will be going to Bentham to visit his aunt.

Back Clive went to Mrs. Belcher and explained to her what his father had said. Mrs. Belcher then said "Clive if your father insists that you visit your aunt then I very reluctantly will have to let you go and terminate your employment." His father continued to insist and a very upset and tearful Mrs Belcher very reluctantly did let Clive go. This was a devastating blow to Clive as once again his father's interfering had ruined a job he loved. This was for Clive the final straw in having his father continue to interfere so detrimentally in his life. So once again he decided to go back down to London and see what life he could make for himself there.

This time as he had some money put by things were a little easier. He had various jobs and moved about quite a bit. From Barnes to Strawberry Hill, Esher, Deptford, Chelsea and then Harrow. During these different jobs Clive would, usually at tea break time, either read palms or read the tea leaves of his work colleagues. He didn't really read the palms but he just used these as a concentration point. However the information that he relayed to his colleagues had them dumb struck as he was able to unite them with deceased parents and friends with accurate descriptions as well as being able to tell them things about themselves.

Spiritual Development
It was while he was working as the Manager in a shoe shop in Ruislip that a lady walked into the shop, a Mrs

Thompson, she was a spiritualist medium and obviously saw something in Clive and his potential. She spoke to him saying that she knew he could see spirit. Clive immediately and vehemently denied this. However she ignored his protestations and continued by saying that he had mediumistic capabilities and suggested that he visit the local Spiritualist Church which was only yards down the road.

Shortly afterwards a gentleman came into the shop and while Clive was helping him on with some shoes he felt a sharp pain in his leg. He asked the gentleman if he had a pain in his leg and he said that he did. Clive told him that he had felt it and the gentleman, who must have been a spiritualist, then said it could be spirit telling Clive. As soon as he said that the pain left Clive.

As a result of these two experiences Clive decided to visit the local spiritualist church. He had no idea what went on at such a church but having pondered on what recently occurred decided to visit anyway. He found the church which was actually a rented hall very easily. When he entered the building, he was met by a Mrs. Fox, who mistakenly said "Oh, you must be the medium". A shocked and agitated Clive said that he definitely was not and promptly sat down at the back of the church. The service started shortly afterwards and the visiting medium started giving messages to people reuniting them with their deceased loved ones. These were all readily accepted and understood.

Then the medium came to Clive with a message telling him that he would become a medium and work for spirit. The medium told him that he must develop the natural gift that he had and find a suitable development circle. The medium then continued with other messages as Clive thought through what had been said to him. After the service Clive was approached by a Mrs. Findlay who invited him to join the development circle where she sat. Clive duly went along and met the circle leader who was Mrs Nan Cowling. She in effect interviewed Clive to see if he was suitable to sit in her development circle.

Nan was well known and highly thought of in spiritualist circles as she had a wealth of knowledge and experience. She lived in Ruislip and had given sittings to many prominent individuals in business and local government. She was a very strict disciplinarian who did not tolerate fools or those with vivid imaginations when it came to her circle work. She ensured that none of her pupils would ever demonstrate on a platform until they were ready and could promote spiritualism in the correct way. She was one of many mediums who never got the recognition for all the good work that she did. In spite of all of these excellent qualities she was a very funny lady who had a very keen sense of humour and would often tell jokes .

After talking to Clive she invited him to sit in her development circle to develop and hone this natural gift. She also told Clive that he would work for spirit and become a medium and work on the platform.

So Clive attended this weekly circle and paid half a crown for the privilege. This was the beginning of his development which would continue for a number of years. The ground rules were that you had to attend without fail each and every week. Sickness or holidays were not an excuse. The meetings were held in the kitchen and everybody sat, in a circle, on hard chairs with their shoeless feet on the cold stone floor. After Clive had attended just a few meetings he was told by

Nan to be half an hour earlier next week although no reason was given.

The following week Clive arrived early as requested. Nan took him into the front room were sat a gentleman who was a complete stranger to Clive. "Right, give that man a reading and don't ask any questions!" she said. So a very nervous Clive gave the man a reading and he responded very positively throughout. At the end she asked the man if he understood everything. "Yes" he replied. "Good" she said, "that will be 30 shillings". The man paid and she quickly put all the money into her apron pocket and let him out. No money went to Clive for giving the sitting, indeed he still had to pay his half a crown to attend the circle.

It was in this circle that Clive's working relationship with his Chinese Guide Woo Wang first surfaced. Although Clive was very much aware of Woo Wang and had in fact seen him quite a few times there had been no exchange between them. During the circle meditation was the first time that Woo Wang started to influence Clive more directly. While Clive was meditating he was aware of the presence of Woo Wang standing beside him and strangely could see that he was speaking but the words and sound were coming out of Clive's mouth. This was very unnerving for a young 17 year-old Clive particularly as it began to occur each time the circle sat.

Clive therefore decided that if Woo Wang wanted to speak using him then he would have to take full control so that Clive would be unaware of what was taking place. From that day forward that was what happened and continues to this day.

One day Clive was invited to go to Old Hatch Manor, which was being used as a spiritualist church, to see a medium. He got there in plenty of time and took his seat in the congregation and waited as the hall filled up, for the service to begin. The start time came and went and there was a bit of a commotion at the back of the church. Shortly afterwards a lady came down to the front and announced that the medium had not arrived and we would have to have a do-it-yourself night. There was a deep sigh of disappointment in the room. But then a lady called Jessie who sat in the same circle as Clive stood up and said "no it's alright, we have Clive here with us tonight and he will do the evening".

This was complete news to Clive as he had not been asked beforehand nor did he approve or want to be volunteered. However now he had no choice and he was invited to come to the front and take the meeting. So a very nervous 17 year-old Clive sat down in a chair at the front. The service started with the usual hymn singing and prayers and then came the time for the demonstration of clairvoyance. Clive nervously closed his eyes to gain his composure. The next thing he new he was "waking up" and had grabbed hold of a jug of water and gulped down the contents. The Chairman then thanked Clive for a truly amazing evening, much to Clive's bewilderment and the service was closed.

Afterwards a Mr. Honas who was a long established member of the church congratulated Clive on a truly wonderful evening saying that Clive was from the "old school" of mediumship and that he must continue to work for spirit. Clive was very puzzled as he did not know what on earth Mr. Honas was on about.

It was then explained to Clive that when he sat down and closed his eyes within a minute or so he was taken over (entranced) by his Chinese Guide – Woo Wang. This guide held the audience spellbound by the accuracy of the messages given and proved survival time and time again. Clive himself has no memory of anything from the moment he sat down to the time he grabbed the jug of water.

Work Commences

Soon the word spread of this successful evening to surrounding churches and Clive started receiving requests to serve churches as the visiting medium. He would demonstrate his gift several times a week in the evenings after he finished work. This would now be his course which has so far already spanned 53 years of serving spirit and people not only all over the UK but also abroad in Japan, America and Germany.

One area that Clive found a little difficult was always going alone to the churches. He had this "thing" that in the Bible Jesus said that "you must go two by two". So Clive wanted a companion who would be there to support and help him in his work. But who?

One day he visited a friend called Charles who lived in Wealdstone. Charles had a friend with him, Harry, and they were celebrating his birthday. Harry was a gardener all his life and worked on Wembley Municipal Park maintaining their gardens. Recently he had been burgled and as a result he felt he could no longer live in that home so he moved into a bed-sit. He still was unsettled and would take any opportunity to be out. Clive therefore offered Harry the chance to come round to his house, when he had a free evening, to watch television. Harry readily agreed. This was the beginning of a life long friendship until Harry passed away in the early 1980s.

On one of these visits the topic of Spiritualism came up and Clive mentioned that he visited churches to demonstrate clairvoyance. Harry asked if he could also come and so they set off together on the next appointment that Clive had. This was in a large house in Ealing where a large room was allocated as the church. The owner who ran the church was a Mrs. Wooster-Mooring a rather overpowering and bossy sergeant major type. When Clive arrived he was told that he must give a message to everybody as they had all paid. It was a long night but all eventually received a message.

When she asked Clive "What is your fee?" Clive said "No, it's alright, there is no fee". Mrs Wooster-Mooring then berated Clive saying "young man, a labourer is worthy of his hire, if you take no fee you will never come and serve this church again! What is your fee?" Clive said "two pounds". A few minutes later she handed him an envelope which he opened when he got home. Inside was one pound ten shillings!

Over the next 8 years or so Clive and Harry would go together to the churches and after a while Harry started to give the addresses on a Sunday. These would broadly be based on a gardening theme as this was his background. Whenever Clive did a trance demonstration, and allowed his Chinese guide Woo Wang to come through and speak, Harry was always there to check that everything was done correctly and also to ensure the safety of the medium. He was fiercely protective of Clive and idolised Woo Wang against whom you could not say a critical word.

As the years rolled by it was clear to Clive that travelling around to all the different churches and meetings was becoming a bit of a struggle for Harry. Although Harry was in his early 70s he looked and behaved as someone who was considerably older. Time would come quite soon when somebody would have to replace Harry but Clive hadn't a clue who this would be or where he would find them.

Harry was also hard of hearing and had one of those old fashioned hearing aids which was prone to whistle from time to time. The aid which was about the size of a box of 20 cigarettes would be placed in the breast pocket of his blazer and a wire with a connected earpiece ran upto his ear. Harry was not very technically minded so he often did not have it set properly and as a result, would on many occasions, only hear snippets of conversations or miss-hear them completely which subsequently led to great confusion.

On one occasion when Clive and Harry visited some friends called Gene and Roger. The subject of healing came up and Harry was very pleased to say that he had been given a healing guide who worked with him. Gene asked "and what is your guides name?" Harry responded with pride "Brown Owl" but he did not speak very clearly so what Gene thought he said was "Brown Ale". "Brown Ale?" Gene asked looking puzzled. As Harry's hearing aid was not set properly he thought she had said Brown Owl so he said "yes that's right." For years to come whenever Gene met Harry she would ask him in all seriousness "How is Brown Ale?" and neither were aware of any misunderstanding.

Spiritual Healing
While attending Ruislip church Clive became more interested in Spiritual Healing and spoke about it with the current healing leader Mr. Silk. He told Clive that Spiritual healing could be administered in many different ways. It could be by the laying on of hands, or absent healing where you send out your thoughts to someone who is unwell or just being a good listener etc.

So Clive started his healing work by allocating time on a Sunday where he could sit quietly at home and send out thoughts to those in need of healing

One particular Sunday Clive arrived at the church and looked truly dreadful. Mr. Silk was rather concerned at his appearance but being astute said, " I imagine that you have spent the day sending out healing thoughts to many people." "I have" said Clive. "Tell me" said Mr. Silk "did you include yourself in your thoughts?" "Oh no, that would be very selfish" responded Clive.

Mr Silk then explained to Clive that the first person he should send out healing thoughts to is himself. The reason being that he has to ensure that he is feeling well so that he can then be used by spirit to help make others better. In other words if Clive is not fit then he will not be a very good channel for the healing energy to flow through him to others.

On one Sunday evening after the service Mr. Silk approached Clive and asked him if he would like to give healing by the laying on of hands to an old lady at the church. Clive was thrilled to be asked and naturally said he would. So he placed his hands on the old lady's shoulders and prayed most earnestly for her to get better, asking for all of his spirit guides and helpers to use him as best they could. After a little while Clive finished his healing and the lady left the church.

The following week Clive went to the church but the old lady was not to be seen. After the service he approached Mr. Silk and asked about her. Mr. Silk replied "Oh she passed away last Sunday night". Clive was distraught, he thought he had in effect killed her off by giving her the healing the previous Sunday. He said to himself if this is the result of my healing work I don't want anything more to do with it.

Some weeks later however when Clive was at his weekly circle the old lady came through another medium present and said thank you to Clive. She said that she was very frightened of dying but the healing she was given gave her the strength to "let go" of this life and pass into the next. This was a very salutary lesson that as a healer you cannot make everyone like a two year old again. You just do the work and let spirit do theirs.

A little while later there were some changes at the church and as a result Clive became uncomfortable there so decided to look for another Spiritualist church. He found one a few miles away at Rayners Lane in Middlesex. There he joined the committee and soon was appointed as President.

2

WOJTEK K. KRAJEWSKI

The Beginning

My parents Zosia Kluczynska and Stefan Krajewski came over to England during the end of World War II. As far as I know they first met in Beaconsfield at a refugee camp and married a little while later. They moved to Streatham and lived in rented accommodation.

The date now is 9th May 1951 at a hospital in Battersea, South London. Zosia Krajewska, who has reached her full term pregnancy, is admitted as her labour has started. A little while later a baby boy is born, me. Wojciech Krzysztof Krajewski, known as Wojtek (pronounced voy-tek). I had an elder brother Andrew who was born on 3rd August 1948 and we all lived in a house in Streatham. I have no real memory of this place at all. My memory seems to start when we all moved to a large house in Birch Grove, Acton, West London.

My earliest recollections are being dressed in a blue one piece "romper" type suite and attached to a harness and being out with my mum. We went to a railway bridge just around the corner on Creffield Road and my mum held me up as the trains, from Ealing Common Station on their way to Ealing Broadway, passed underneath and I waved at the drivers. Some waved back which made me very excited but some did not.

The only other real memories I have is my mother and father being out a lot and not seeing much of them. I now know that they were working all hours of the day to pay the mortgage and various other bills. There were also other people in the house (lodgers) who I did not know. My mother spent a lot of time either in bed or away (hospital). My brother and I were totally unaware that this was all due to her progressive illness of stomach cancer.

My brother and I were sent away several times on holiday in the summer to Henley-on-Thames to a place called Fawley Court. This was a Polish catholic boarding school run by the Marian Fathers but became a holiday home in the Summer holidays. The days there as a young boy of 6 and 7 were not good as I felt very homesick indeed. We would wait anxiously for a visit of my father on a Sunday afternoon and would spend hours looking down the long driveway to see if he was coming. He always did but it seemed he was always much later than expected. My mother presumably was having another stay in hospital at this time and my parents felt that it was best for us boys to be away. I hated this place as did my brother and we spent many hours walking round the grounds crying and being thoroughly miserable.

When at home there was not any laughter and fun that I can really remember. My father always seemed very distant and preoccupied with his own thoughts. I remember Christmas's where presents were very scarce and those that were received were not what I had hoped for. Christmas dinner, in spite of the effort that clearly had been made, did not really seem much different from other days. Money was as ever very tight.

My mother had been away from home again for some time and my dad had been more agitated than usual. An aunt was staying with us as well as some family friends. It was in the evening on 21st February 1959 and we were all sitting in the front room. The phone rang. My father answered. There was a long pause. He then said something in a very solemn voice to the person on the phone while the others in the room looked resigned and listened intently. He put the phone down and said something to everybody. I did not know or understand what it was but everyone fell silent in deep thought for what seemed ages. Some shed quiet tears. I just sat there unsure of what had happened but knew it was very serious and sad. My mum had just passed away. I was 7 and Andrew was 10 years old.

Life without Mum

Things as you can imagine were in turmoil for my dad, brother and me. I remember going to the funeral parlour to say "goodbye" to my mum. She was in her coffin dressed in black but just did not look like the mum I had known. I was ushered to an alter in the viewing room and told to say some prayers. I knelt down and far from praying I just cried uncontrollably. After some time my dad came over and lifted me up by my arm and said it was time to say goodbye. He told me to kiss my mother. I lent over the coffin and kissed her on the forehead. It was a shock as she felt cold and clammy and not the warm and affectionate person I had known. On the day of the funeral there were no tears from me, that was left for the others present. Perhaps I was just exhausted by it all now, but many tears flowed in the days that were to follow.

There were some friends of the family who we referred to as Auntie Lola and Uncle Marion that we boys liked very much and visited quite often. They were always very generous to us and after my mother passed away they wanted to adopt us. My father however did not approve of this. So nothing happened, although it did put some friction in their relationship and as a result we did not see so much of them.

During this difficult time my father tried to bring life back to some kind of normality but he had great difficulty coping with it all. I remember that as a treat he would buy "Mary Baker Sponge Mix" which was a prepared cake mix, and attempt to bake us a cake. It was a good job we had strong teeth! We also ate quite a few burnt meals and I remember lifting the lid off a saucepan, he had put away, to find a whole load of healthy and well fed maggots.

My dad then started going out, usually on a Friday or Saturday night. He would always be smartly dressed and I distinctly remember what to me was an overpowering smell of aftershave. Sometimes he would take us to the cinema to see a film and then slip out virtually as soon as we were seated and leave us to watch it on our own. He just told us he had to meet someone and left Andrew in charge to make sure we got home after the film finished. Sometimes he would leave us on our own at home. All very mysterious to a young mind.

Then one day he told us that he was going to bring a visitor to see us, a lady. Who she was or where she came from or indeed how she knew my dad remained a mystery. However she did come, and Andrew and I were introduced. I was very shy but did like her and for weeks to come I always referred to her as "the lady". Some time later they were married so I now had a step mum. I called her by a pet name "Nunia" as I just could not call her mum, it somehow did not seem right, as if I did, then it would be very disloyal to my birth mother.

Nunia

Nunia was a great mum as anyone who takes on two young boys is really letting themselves in for quite a challenging time. She was a great cook and we ate well everyday. On top of running the house she was also an outworker for years and sewed some sort of Lapland jackets on an old Singer treadle sewing machine. She also developed a number of private clients for whom she sewed bespoke garments. She worked into the night often sowing and I can still remember the sound of her treddling away when I was in bed. Some years later this sound was replaced by a fast "whiz" when my dad bought an electric sewing machine.

It was clear that she loved both boys but she got on better with me than my brother Andrew. A little later on Christmas Eve my father told us, in what seemed to me to be a very solemn voice that we would have to be very careful and helpful to Nunia because she was, and he used the Polish word, "w ciazy". I did not know what this meant but assumed, because of his serious tone, that it was some terrible illness and promptly burst into tears. It was then explained to me that this mystery word meant that Nunia was in fact pregnant. On June 30th 1963 my half sister Grazyna (Gina) was born.

Family life continued I guess very much like any other family with the usual ups and downs and the years passed by. In about 1970 my father was given, by my Grandad (Nunia's dad) a Vauxhall Viva van which had side windows added. Grandad owned a garage called Prom Motors in Kirkcaldy, Scotland which was on the

Esplanade and looked out to the sea. I spent some very enjoyable holidays there. My dad learnt to drive and passed his test. He was really proud to have done so and now had independence to go about much more freely. He loved his car and could frequently be found tinkering with the interior upgrading the furnishings.

In 1971 he drove Nunia and my sister to Holyhead in Anglesey for a holiday where they were to stay with some friends. Before they left I said my usual "goodbyes" but this time for some reason (which became clear later) when I said goodbye to my dad I jokingly shook his hand for a long time making a big thing about him going and said "do send me a post-card, after all you will be away such a long time." He looked into my eyes and just smiled and grinned at my unusual "over the top" display of affection particularly as he was due to be back in a couple of days.

A few days later on the Sunday he was driving back home alone. I was at home and happen to be looking out of my bedroom window when I saw a police "panda" car slowly pull up outside our house. The policeman inside the car gathered some papers and then got out of his car. He headed straight for our garden gate, opened it and started walking up our path. I felt great trepidation as I rushed down the stairs and opened the front door just as he pressed the doorbell. It was about 4pm on Sunday afternoon.

There stood a very solemn looking policeman who asked me if any family or relatives of a Mr. Stefan Krajewski lived at this address. I said, "yes, I am his son". The policeman then said, without any forewarning or tact, "Your father was found dead in his car in a lay-by just outside of Rugby". I jumped backwards in shock and disbelief unable to really take in what had

39

just been said. My mind was racing all over the place at a 100 miles an hour. The policeman gave me some details and left. I immediately rang my brother who lived a few miles away in Acton and he made his way to the house. While I was waiting for my brother to arrive my mind drifted back to the time I said good bye to him. Now I understood that final long farewell to him.

This devastating news was made even worse when the phone rang, a few hours later. I answered. It was Nunia and she asked in a cheery voice "Has dad got home?" I had to then tell her the awful news which she in turn had to relay to my 8 year-old sister.

The next few years were a struggle particularly for Nunia who had so much to cope with. Financial difficulties, running the house, sewing, looking after my sister and me, dealing with the few tenants that we had, some of whom had their own problems which they shared with her. How much help I was at that time I do not really know but we seemed to muddle through.

I had wanted to leave home and "find my feet" for some time, but felt that in the circumstances it was not yet right to do so. Indeed I felt that the time would never be right but it was something that had to be done.

The years rolled by and at age 23 I finally, with very mixed feelings and tears running down my face, left home and moved to Harrow to be closer to my work. I shared a house with three girls, Rosemarie and Annemarie who were twins and their friend Camilla. It was quite an eye opener in many ways as I was still a pretty shy person.

My future?
When at age twelve I was asked what work I wanted to do in life. At that time it ranged from being a doctor,

surgeon, vet, policeman, social services (particularly where children were involved), priest or something to do with helping others. One of the problems that I knew I would have to conquer, if I followed any of these, was not to get emotionally involved which I knew would be very difficult for me. At that time there were seemingly two routes in life that I could take. One was to become a catholic priest, the other was marriage and work. Both had some appeal to me but for very different reasons.

I was brought up as a Catholic and this was to give me a set of strong religious and moral beliefs. I guess it did for my first 14 years but then as puberty and thinking for myself set in I began to question some of these teachings. I have nothing against the Catholic faith but I concluded that it was just not for me.

In my late teens we had a Polish priest come to live in our home who had a keen interest in youth and what made us all tick. He had in fact written a number of educational come informative books about sex and what we as youngsters should be aware of as we matured. He also carried out counselling for single and pre and post married couples. It always seemed to me to be very odd that here was someone who, certainly in theory, had no experience of sexual relationships, particularly within marriage yet was advising those with various sexual problems how they should conduct themselves. The experience of having a priest live within our home with all the very different things this entailed certainly put me off the priesthood.

So that left marriage then. Now marriage can be a very happy constitution and I have nothing against it particularly as I love children. Within marriage there must be love, trust, respect, tolerance, balance and many more good characteristics. But in the sphere of people I knew and increasingly came into contact with I found very few marriages which, in my meaning of the word, were truly loving and happy. Instead there was bickering, frustration, anger and resignation that this was just the way it is. This would be most unfortunate and disastrous particularly where young children were involved.

I vowed never to marry unless those good characteristics mentioned above were present. I had had a few relationships with girls over the years and two could potentially have led to marriage. But I knew that they were not right so it was better that they ceased before we embarked on a long and bumpy road of unhappiness.

When I left school I still did not have a real idea of a career path that I would like to follow. So I signed up with a few employment agencies to see what they could offer me and as a result started by first job at Mercantile Credit Company in Holborn, London as a Documentation Clerk. To actually get paid a monthly salary directly into my new bank account was certainly a very pleasant and grown up experience.

I had been at the company about 6 months or so and was invited one Friday lunchtime to join some colleagues in the local pub which was close to the office. It was late autumn and drizzling so many people wore coats. I had a little work that I wanted to finish before lunch so told them that I would join them shortly.

I finished my work and went over to the pub. I had never been there before so did not know the layout or who from work went there. As I opened the door it was clear the place was pretty well packed out and mostly with people I recognised from the office. At the same time I happen to notice a free standing coat stand by the door begin to slowly move and start to fall. What had actually happened was that many people had hung up their coats but just on one side of the stand thereby making it very unstable. The draft from the door must have been sufficient to unbalance it.

Now I had not touched it at all but I was the one closest to it. It continued to fall and to my horror it was heading straight toward the back of one of the Directors and all to quickly it banged into him which seemed to cause a reflex jerk of his right arm in which he had a full pint of beer. This resulted in the colleague standing opposite him to be drenched in most of the contents.

Everybody turned to look at me with very accusing and disapproving stares. I was mortified and started to scrabble about on the floor picking up the various assortment of coats. The situation was made even worse when various items fell out of some of the pockets and rolled about on the floor. I think my prospects at the company had now been sealed.

It was shortly after this episode that I joined the Shipbuilding Industry Training Board (SITB) in South Harrow, Middlesex as their statistical assistant. I stayed there for some four years and then decided that it was time to move into the commercial marketplace.

3

FIRST MEETING – RAYNERS LANE SPIRITUALIST CHURCH 1976

I was now working in Wembley for Whitton James Ltd, a company that manufactured "auto-pasting reel stands". These could hold up to three enormous rolls of paper that were then fed into the print machines used by the newsprint organisations, which at that time were still based in Fleet Street, to produce newspapers. My title was "Management Trainee" and in theory I was being groomed for greater things in the future. But the company was going through some very hard times and after just over two years in June 1976 I was made redundant and received a small redundancy payout of about £300. The summer in 1976 was one of the hottest on record so I decided to enjoy these months and find a job in the autumn. I would stay in bed while the others in the house scurried around in the morning getting ready for work. At about 9.30am I would get up, have a very leisurely breakfast, mope around a bit then go down to the Harrow Leisure Centre and spend time in the gym followed by a sauna. I would drift back home in the late afternoon and sometimes prepare a meal for the household.

In the autumn I started my job search but did not really know what I was looking for. I went for various interviews and did in fact get a few job offers but I turned them all down as I felt that they were not suitable, not that I had the faintest idea what would be suitable. Christmas came and went and money was now becoming increasingly tight and thoughts of selling my beloved Skoda S100 (a car I bought new in 1972 for the grand sum of £736 on the road) of necessity started to loom in my mind.

More months passed by but finally in April 1977 I started a new job for Allied Business Systems (a member of the Trafalgar House Group) based in Green Park, London. This was a computer company selling Mini Computers, (all a bit high tech at the time) and my title was Pre-Sales Systems Analyst. No, I didn't know what it really meant either. However, I stayed with the same company, through various sales and management positions, takeovers, mergers etc for over 23 years.

Before I started my new job the twins who I shared with moved on to live in Cambridge and new people moved in (Kevin and Sharon) although we all still kept in touch and saw each other from time to time. On one of their visits they mentioned that their parents, who lived in Rayners Lane, had been to this "funny little church". It was situated behind and under the main shops in a large garage. Apparently it was a Spiritualist Church. This got my attention as I had always been interested in the paranormal.

They asked me if I fancied going one day and I readily agreed. Some weeks later I went with Kevin, out of curiosity, to see what this little church was all about. We arrived at the back of the shops and made our way along a very uneven and massively pot-holed road come path. We went through one of the garage doors, as the other was locked shut, wondering what on earth to expect inside. What a surprise, the interior had been truly transformed with a rostrum, organ, carpets and chairs, a small kitchen area and another tiny little room with a couple of chairs and a folding table. There was a really friendly atmosphere and the place had a real "buzz" about it.

We sat down towards the middle of the church on the right hand side and waited for the service to begin. We had no idea what to expect other than there was supposed to be a medium who would convey messages from people who had "died". At 8.00pm the organist started playing by peddling his feet on the bellows of the old organ and two people walked down the aisle of the church.

The first was a suited and portly gentleman in his 60s whose most distinguishing feature was his unique hairstyle. It was obvious that he was very thin or bald on top but he had swept his hair, which was white at its roots but black thereafter, from the back of his neck to the front of his head. In fact his parting was not in the normal place on the side of the head, it was in fact, almost right at the base of his neck! The whole structure was expertly pinned into a rigid form by a series of very visible clips. This was the medium who was well known within the spiritualist movement in London and the Home Counties and had spent many years working in different churches. His name was Billy Elton (he passed into spirit in 2006) the then President of Aylesbury Spiritualist Church which he had founded.

Following behind was the chairperson and again I was drawn to his hairstyle. It looked like a cross between Frank Zappa's (a pop star of the day) and a wild Afro crop which stuck out from his head like a wild bush. He was dressed in a pink shirt with a frilly centrepiece and cuffs. The skin-tight trousers were Rupert Bear in style with a loud cross check. This was my first view of Clive Daniels who was the President of the church. Now I was brought up in the Catholic church (although I lapsed when I was 14) so I was used to a much more formal dress code by the clergy and seeing this was very odd to me at that time.

The service started with a welcome to the congregation and introduction of the visiting medium, followed by the first hymn. We were then asked to send out "healing thoughts" to all those we knew who were sick or suffering. I had no idea what this meant. Were we supposed to write the information down on a piece of paper and then someone would collect them to send off somewhere? What was this all about? I hadn't a clue in those days.

We had another hymn and then the Chairman announced that this was the part of the service where the medium would demonstrate his gift of clairvoyance and if he should come to us then we should answer him with a clear voice, as this would improve the link with spirit. I was not sure what this really meant either. Kevin and I looked at each other in a very bemused way.

The medium then stood up and started to demonstrate. He seemed to talk to the wall of the building on his right side as if he was having a conversation with an invisible person. Then he turned to face the congregation and spoke to someone and relayed the information he got from this invisible person. Bizarre! Now to my astonishment and amusement the person the medium was talking to said they understood exactly what the medium was telling them. Again Kevin and

I looked at each other and we started giggling because this was all surely quite crazy wasn't it. This went on as the medium spoke to each new person in the congregation and we continued to grin and giggle. I thought this whole thing was a complete load of nonsense and farcical. The people here in the church must all be nuts. Kevin and I could hardly contain our giggles which were now consuming us both.

Then I looked at the Chairman and his eyes were fixed at me with a very disapproving and rebuking glare. I immediately blushed and looked down to the floor. My giggling ceased. Every now and again I looked up at him and he still had that disapproving stare at me which seemed to penetrate my whole being. I felt most uncomfortable. It was only some years later that Clive told me that, if I had continued to giggle and grin, he would have stopped the service there and then and told me that if I could not respect this way of worship then I would have to leave the church.

The evening was coming to a close and the Chairman said to the medium that the next message would be the last. Great I thought, I would be able to get out of this place. But what happened next shook me and badly. The medium looked directly at me. He pointed and said that he wanted to speak to that young man, me. My heart started to pound excessively and I turned bright red, my face felt on fire! He told me things that I could relate to very much and meant something to me but my "logical" mind was telling me this cannot be right as how could he possibly know these things.

After my message the service concluded with another hymn followed by the church notices and we were all invited to stay for a cup of tea and a chat. We declined and scurried out quickly.

I left the church that night shaken by the message I was given and decided that surely it was all a load of rubbish. Must be some sort of mind reading or telepathy I thought. But I would go again next week just to prove it to be so. I went again next week and again I got a message that I understood. I kept asking myself, but how does the medium know so much about me and those in my family who had passed away. Never mind I thought, I would come again just to disprove it all. This was my introduction to Spiritualism which has continued so far for over 30 years.

4

MY SPIRITUAL AWAKENING

So I started going to the church every Thursday to the 8.00pm service that lasted an hour. Following the service people were invited to stop for a cup of tea and a "natter". I never stopped for tea afterwards as I made a mad dash home so that I could watch "The Sweeny" on TV which started at 9.00pm. So for an hour I had the peace and tranquillity of the church followed by an hour of violent mayhem on TV. The two things don't quite blend together well do they?

My confidence slowly grew at the church and I now wanted to receive a message from the visiting medium. The problem was how could I get the medium to notice me. Usually the medium gave between 6 to 8 messages and as often there were over 30 people in the congregation then the odds were against me. One tactic I used, when the medium would come off the rostrum and walk amongst the congregation, was to sit in the aisle seat with one of my legs sticking out into the aisle. Then "accidentally" as they walked by I would make sure that they collided with my leg. Contact was therefore made and more often than not the medium would give me the next message. Success!

Also in those days when I arrived for a service I would quickly check out the hymns. If they had four verses then that was o.k. If they had more I was annoyed because then those extra verses could have been the time taken away from my message. Occasionally they put up a hymn with 4 verses and 4 choruses, which almost gave me a seizure. I would rarely come on a Sunday night because there was an Address and I had no intention to listen to someone droning on and on about things spiritual. In those days it was just the messages that interested me.

Every now and again I received a message from the medium. Some messages were more readily understood than others but there was a strange reoccurring theme that kept coming up. This was that I would work for spirit and had the gift of healing. Now what working for spirit actually meant I did not know but if it involved travelling round all the different churches giving up my free time then it was definitely a no no.

However, every now and again the President of the church, Clive Daniels, would be there on a Thursday or Sunday. Quite often he chaired the meeting but now I had learnt my lesson and behaved appropriately. Even more surprisingly I had started to stay after the services for a cup of tea and a chat. Occasionally I would speak to Clive Daniels who was very popular and always had people around him. There was something intriguing about him, I did not know what it was but I was somehow drawn to him.

A few weeks later I am again at the church for the Thursday evening service. I do not know who the medium is so just waited to see. The music starts and two people walk down to the rostrum. One is Clive and the other a lady but this time Clive sits in the medium's seat and the lady sits in the chairman's. I had never seen Clive work so thought "this will be interesting".

The service started in the usual way and then we came to the clairvoyant part of the evening. The Chairman starts to tell us the usual introduction to the clairvoyance but then looks at Clive who remains seated and seems to have fallen asleep. She looked a little surprised and tells us that we are lucky because we are to have Woo Wang visit us tonight. Who the blazes is Woo Wang I thought, what's going on. With that a loud high pitched whine like voice comes from Clive's mouth and says "My name is Woo Wang and I come to you from the world of spirit". Oh sh*t I thought. What the hell is going on here. He stood up keeping his eyes closed throughout and then started giving messages to people and it was clear that they understood them very well. This Woo Wang fellow was very stern sounding and took no messing from anyone. I really hoped he did not come to speak to me and to ensure this I sunk into my seat in a vain attempt to make myself smaller.

"Last message" said the chairman. Oh good it's nearly all over and I will be able to relax. "I want to speak to that young man at the back!" Woo Wang said very loudly and curtly, pointing in my direction. Oh hell that's me. "Hello" I said with nervous hesitation. I could feel the veins in my neck pulsating wildly as my heart raced out of control. Woo Wang then proceeded, to what I felt was a "no holds barred" public berating on various matters about me. It was so embarrassing yet it was so very accurate. He pointed out the errors of my ways in no uncertain terms in a very stern and disapproving voice. After the service I quickly left without the "tea chat". I vowed never to return, I was so humiliated and in public too.

I festered for a week or two after this "public assassination" and my emotions swung from being very angry to being disappointed with myself and finally admitting that this Woo Wang person did in fact have a very deserving point. So perhaps it was time to change.

So I continued to go to the church in Rayners Lane and started to get slowly involved in some of the other activities that they held. I remember that they had an "Open Circle" on a Monday night where people could go if they wished to learn more about Spiritualism and possibly start to develop any mediumistic abilities.

I decided to go and see what this was all about. One particular night, which stuck out in my mind, was when Clive was present. The lady who was running the group said that as Clive was here tonight he would let his Chinese Guide – Woo Wang come through and speak to the group and then we would have the opportunity to ask questions. As I had had a rather sobering encounter with this Woo Wang character last time and not seen him since I was a little apprehensive but also intrigued how the evening would go.

The evening started with an opening prayer and then we were told just to sit back and relax and send our thoughts out to Clive while he allowed himself to go into trance. There were about 20 of us sitting in a circle and we had some subdued lighting so we could still see pretty well.

Clive closed his eyes and seemed, slowly, to sink into himself. After about a minute that familiar high pitched whine came out of his mouth "My name is Woo Wang and I come to you from the world of spirit." I focussed on Clive very intently to see if I could check whether he was faking this trance work. I listened intently to what was being said, again to see if I could find any flaws in the logic etc. I could not but I would keep on trying.

After a short talk by Woo Wang the lady running the evening said that it was now our opportunity to ask any questions. People did start asking what to me were rather facile and mundane questions like, "what is the world of spirit like, do you meet your relatives there, have you met God etc etc". Everybody accepted the answers very readily without questioning even when Woo Wang gave them the opportunity to come back with any supplementary questions. They all to me seemed a bit overwhelmed with Woo Wang and held him in very high esteem.

OK. Time for my question so I raised my hand and the circle leader signalled to me to speak. My question was, "Woo Wang, how can you convince me that what we are witnessing here tonight is true trance and not a load of old codswallop?"

There was a stunned and prolonged silence. Everyone turned and looked at each other first, some open mouthed, in shock and disbelief. Then they all turned to look at me, this very rude, brash and young ill-mannered person who had the audacity to ask such a disgraceful question. If looks could kill I would have been dead several times over that night.

The only person who remained composed and unaffected was Woo Wang who chuckled to himself and replied "I have never been called codswallop before." He went onto say, "Mr Gentleman I cannot convince you of anything. If you think what I say is good then hold onto it. If you think that it is rubbish then just throw it away. But make sure that in the piece you throw away is not the seed of an even greater truth. I would suggest that you follow me from place to place to see my work.

Check that I am consistent in what I say, see if you can catch me out."

That was the beginning of a long association with Woo Wang which still continues to this day. I have devoted a chapter to him later on in this book which will give a greater insight to this individual and his work. By the way, after all these years I have still been unable to catch him out.

By now I had become a "regular" at the church and had even started to come to the Sunday evening services. I would listen intently to the addresses some of which I thought were good others not so. I was also beginning to get to know Clive better and spent more time chatting to him, usually about things spiritual. Quite often after the Thursday service we would go for a meal to the "Mad Hatter" in Harrow it was a very popular place and served desserts "to die for". I was gradually getting closer to Clive.

He was at that time either serving a church or taking a group in someone's house virtually every day of the week. All proceeds going to the church to pay the weekly rent of £25 and also to try and amass a building fund for a new church at some time, way in the future. I do not know quite how it happened but after one of our chats I found that I had sort of been engineered come volunteered myself to rewiring the church.

A few weeks later I had somehow become Clive's new "booking secretary". This meant that all future bookings would be through me and I had total control of his movements.

It was also round about this time that he suggested to me that I should accompany him to some of the churches so that I could see how different they all were. I agreed.

Shortly after I realised that again I had somehow now become "his driver" too.

Most evenings now meant a dash home after work, quick shower, change, some food if time allowed and then drive over to Clive to pick him up for his evening appointment. I did enjoy going out with Clive to the various churches and groups and found it a very educational and at times emotional experience. To see the joy on people's faces when they were reunited by those who had passed into the world of spirit was truly humbling. Depending where these meetings took place governed the time we got back to our respective homes, but it was usually after 11.00pm.

This routine now became my life and I was enjoying it. Then Clive's next subtle step was "inadvertently" put to me. Clive told me that it was important to him, that when he served a church or group, particularly as he demonstrated in trance, that he had someone he could rely and trust to be close to hand. He said it would be better therefore if I could sit on the platform with him as he could "draw on my energy" more easily. Again somehow I now found myself sitting on the platform looking out at the sea of faces in the congregations.

This went on for some months and now it was me who said that while I do not mind being on the platform, to just sit there like the proverbial lemon made me feel daft. I think I played straight into his hands. "Well" he said, "why don't you just open in prayer." Within weeks I was not only opening but also closing in prayer. Anyone think there is a bit of a trend developing here?

Again this new routine carried on for a few months and I was growing a bit more in confidence (or was it ego) so one bright day I said to Clive that I would like to give the address at the next Sunday service. Clive asked me if I was sure and I said yes of course I was. After all there cannot really be very much to it, can there?

The following Sunday we arrive at Wembley Spiritualist Church and were greeted by the Mediums Secretary a Miss Brown. She was a small, slightly stooped, elderly bespectacled lady who spoke with what to me sounded like a very posh voice. "Hello Claive, (she always added the "a" in his name") so very nice to see you" she said. Clive explained to her that I would be giving the address that night and with that she very critically looked me up and down with a slightly disapproving gaze. You could see her mind ticking over and I felt the thoughts were not good.

"Now young man we do like a good address at this church, at least twenty minutes," she instructed me. My confidence and ego vanished instantly and I now dreaded the service starting. But 6.30 pm came all to soon and we were off. The chairman collected us from the medium's room and we made our way into the church and climbed up a few steps onto the rather rickety rostrum. I sat down heavily. I was now beginning to regret my decision to give my first address particularly as the prayer and hymns seem to rush by so quickly this night.

Then that dreaded time came and the chairman said to the congregation that I would now address them. Where is that hole in the ground when you need it most? There was no escape. I had to get up. So with my chest thumping and my face crimson red, looking as if it was about to explode, I stood up. Only to find that my legs had suddenly and inexplicably turned into jelly and I started to shake uncontrollably. I grabbed the front of the rostrum in a vain attempt to steady myself but the only effect was that the whole rostrum now also started shaking. Even the long stemmed flowers in the vases were loosing their petals with the vibrations. Both the chairman and Clive gave me a very anxious look, as they too both wobbled in their chairs as a result of my shaking.

There was a long pause, then I took a deep breath and as Christmas was only a few weeks away I chose the topic of Tolerance to speak about. I said that at this time of year people tend to be more tolerant towards each other and a bit more forgiving because it is Christmas. But that it was us that created this more tolerant atmosphere and us that let it go so quickly after Christmas and that the world would be a better place if we could keep this tolerance all year and not just save it for Christmas. That was the gist of what I said. It lasted no more than two minutes and I collapsed into my seat. The rostrum now stopped shaking. The chairman looked at me in complete bewilderment. Fortunately before Clive started demonstrating his clairvoyance he expanded on what I said and mentioned that it was my first address.

The following day Clive is sitting at home and the phone rings. Clive answers and a voice says "Hello Claive, it's Miss Brown here." "Hello Miss Brown" said Clive. "Now Claive I thought that I should ring you to say that we did all very much enjoy your service last night and do look forward to your next visit, but please do not bring that young man with you again." Clive was infuriated and told Miss Brown politely but very firmly that if he cannot bring me with him, to the church, next time, then she had better cancel the remainder of his bookings. This she very reluctantly did. He also asked her to reflect on what the topic of my very short address was but unfortunately she could not recall it. Clive therefore reminded her that the subject was tolerance and where was her and the church's tolerance to a new speaker. The call ended abruptly.

When Clive told me about this my confidence, such that it was, had completely vanished and it was some 18 months before I gave my next address. Fortunately I had now progressed a little more and although very nervous I managed a lot better. A few years later we both served Wembley Spiritualist Church again. The address was now upto standard and there were no complaints, on the contrary there was much praise.

5

APPORTS

The year now is 1980 and I had been steadily putting money away every month into four different building societies with the hopeful view of being granted a mortgage by one of them when I needed it. My hunt for a flat had now begun and I started receiving specification sheets, most of which were totally unsuitable on grounds of price, location, or general amenities. However one sheet came through for a flat in Jasmine Gardens, South Harrow. It was very expensive and really beyond my capabilities although it did look ideal. The cost was £21,000!

I ignored it as it was just too much. That was till Clive saw it and said why don't you make an appointment to view. This we did and we both liked it very much and our earlier thoughts on the property were confirmed. But I just could not afford it. Clive suggested that I make a cheeky offer of what I could afford. I said I could realistically only afford £19,000 and they would never except that. But he pursued it further with me and eventually a week or two later I rang the agent and offered £19,000. The offer, to my surprise and relief, was accepted and a few months later in July 1980 Clive helped me move in.

With all the turmoil and confusion of moving it would

not be unusual for things to get misplaced. But strange things started to happen. I had only been in about a week and I distinctly remembered placing a gold ring with the family crest into my desk drawer before the move. However when I looked into this very same drawer now, the ring was not there, even after I had tipped out the contents on the carpet and sifted through it. Strangely I was not concerned and frantic but felt that it would just turn up somewhere.

A day or so later I had just come out of the shower having washed my hair. I went into the room where my desk was as my hairdryer was in a box on the window ledge. As I reached out for it I noticed to my surprise that my gold ring was just sitting there on top of the box. That is strange I thought, I don't remember putting it there. Perhaps in all the confusion of moving I had, in fact, put it there but just could not remember. I left it at that.

Now it is a few days later and I am getting ready for work. The only mirror that, at that time, I had in the flat was on the inside of an old wardrobe. I had this open as I was putting on my tie and as I slid the knot upto my neck and arched my head backwards my eye caught a glimpse of something shinny on top of the wardrobe. So I got up on my toes and reached out and picked this object up. It was a gold sovereign ring identical to one I had seen Clive wear on several occasions.

Now Clive is a boy for his jewellery and had quite a few bits and pieces. I didn't like this particular ring as I said that it was a typical "barrow boys ring". But how on earth did it get on top of my wardrobe. Various thoughts came into my head. He must have placed it there when he was here last or worse still he had a key to my flat and came in when I was out.

I took the ring to work with me and at lunchtime I rang Clive. I asked him if he could please tell me the date on that sovereign ring that he had. He asked me why I was asking and I said I was just curious. He hung up and went upstairs to his bedroom and picked up the extension and I could hear him rummaging through his jewellery box and mutter begrudgingly away to himself. He rummaged and rummaged and eventually came back to the phone and said rather desperately "I can't find it!"

"I am not surprised because I have got it here" I said. There then ensued a rather difficult conversation with Clive accusing me of having pinched it from his jewellery box when I last visited and me accusing him of having an illicit key to my flat and placing the ring on top of my wardrobe. We both pleaded our respective innocence but logic told us both that surely someone was lying. I even thought that if he had not got a key then he somehow must have catapulted the ring through my letterbox. But how he managed the trajectory to defy physics and go round two right hand corners and end up higher than its starting point had me baffled. Was something else going on here?

Now this was time when I was getting more and more involved in working for spirit but I continued to question spiritualism and indeed my closer friendship with Clive. My mind was a bit all over the place and I was being pulled in several directions. Part of me was saying go with the work for spirit and allow your closeness to Clive to take its natural course. Another part of me needed more "evidence" of spirit and surely getting closer to Clive would be very wrong. I was in somewhat of a turmoil and quandary.

I returned Clive's ring the next time I saw him and

an uneasy "truce" about the matter was agreed. We were both a little uncomfortable. A few days later I pick Clive up from home as we had another Sunday service to go to. After the service I had to drive past my flat to take Clive home so I asked him if he wanted to come in for a coffee. He agreed. Bear in mind that he had not been there since the "ring" incident and I had not been to his home other than to pick him up for the service.

As I am opening the door of the flat Clive says to me "something of mine has been put here". "What?" I said. "Some jewellery" he replied. Here we go again I thought. I will keep very close to Clive just in case he plants something. We walked into my flat together and went into the lounge. "It's in here somewhere". Clive said. Fine I thought but don't let him out of your sight. We walked around the room looking on the table and display cabinet. Nothing. Clive walked towards my stereo unit which was on the floor by the window. I was still right next to him. Then he pointed to the floor in the space behind the record deck and the window. Lying there was his gold neck chain which had been laid out but with a loose knot in the middle.

To us both this was a surprise for two reasons. One was that this jewellery apport had happened again and secondly was the loose knot spirit telling us that we should indeed be together. We had coffee and I took Clive home.

The following day Clive is sitting at home during his lunch break. I am in my office at Maple Cross, Rickmansworth. The letterbox on Clive's front door rattles. Clive thinks to himself that the postman is very late today and goes to pickup the mail. He opens the door to the porch and there on the floor are lying a set of keys. I have a spare set of keys for my flat in my desk. That evening he rings me at home and tells me about these keys. I check my desk. The keys are missing. I ask Clive to come over so that we could just check that they unlocked my door. As soon as I said this we both knew what the answer was going to be. He came over, and yes, we were both right. Another sign that we should be together?

Over the next couple of months various bits of Clive's jewellery would end up in my flat much to his annoyance. He did however make a fatal mistake one night when we were discussing this, saying that it was rather odd that it is only gold that is taken from his house and never anything with diamond in it. Yes you have guessed it, several days later he rings me to say his favourite diamond ring has gone missing. This was a ring that Clive had made with 33 small diamonds. Why 33? Well Clive had some daft notion years ago that he would die at the same age as Jesus so he had the ring specially made. He was at this time already 8 years out of date. Some days later the ring does turn up in one of my coffee cups that is hanging up in my kitchen.

I can truly understand that you may feel that all this whizzing about of jewellery and keys from Clive's house to my flat could just not be possible. If I was reading about it I would very probably feel the same. But all I can say is that this is what happened and indeed I have only highlighted a few of the occurrences. Why did it all happen? Well, it was great evidence to me in the power of spirit and also a big signal that Clive and I being together was also right. But would others see that too?

6

OUR WORK TOGETHER BEGINS

We were now working together for spirit at quiet a heavy and increasing pace. In 1980 we carried out 99 appointments and we peaked in 1984 with 145 appointments. I was also taking bookings upto two years in advance. All of this as well as both of us being in full time jobs. Our normal weekly schedule would typically include a couple of services and/or a few trance groups. We both enjoyed the work and were motivated by the joy and happiness that it gave to those who came and those we served.

At the Sunday services I would give the address and Clive would demonstrate clairvoyance, while at the trance sittings it was always Woo Wang who spoke through Clive. I racked up many miles on the car and am forever grateful to my employer as it was a company car and without which we would not have been able to do so much.

Initially our work took us all around the London and Home Counties serving many different churches. Some were purpose built churches others were hired halls and even on one occasion the services were held in a council flat. The venue was not in itself important but the atmosphere and people who were running it and those who came most certainly were.

Those that attend services can be very diverse from the mildly interested, curious, recently bereaved, total skeptics etc. In other words from all walks of life and backgrounds each with their own reasons for attending. As a Spiritualist medium Clive's job was to, and always is, to prove survival beyond the death of the physical body. My job is to support him as is his to support me when I give an address.

Sometimes when driving to serve a church we have really not felt in the mood particularly when it has been a church where we have not felt comfortable working before. Often our reservations are confirmed upon arrival but we have been booked so we must fulfil the engagement. However on these occasions there is so often one message which is the highlight of the night which has really meant something special to the recipient and this makes our journey so worthwhile.

There have been quiet a few times after the service when people have approached Clive to thank him for the message he gave (sometimes years earlier) and told him that it has changed their life for the better. These are truly humbling moments which give us refreshed strength to continue the work and at the same time tell us that we must put our "not felt in the mood" times to one side, as the next message given could make such a beneficial difference to somebody's life.

On one of our visits we were booked to serve a new church in North London. Although we had the address we were struggling to find the exact location. I would always drive so Clive had to navigate. This at times led to all sorts of confusion because Clive is dyslexic. So he would be looking at our trusty dog eared A to Z and say turn next right but would be waving his left arm indicating to turn left. By the time we had sorted out the confusion we had missed the turning and were off in the wrong direction again. Today fortunately we have Satellite Navigation in the car which to us has been a Godsend and makes for a much more hassle free and peaceful journey.

Eventually we got to the address but it was a Café? I got out the car and out of the side door of the adjoining building emerged a very black lady with brilliant white teeth. She greeted us very warmly and led us down a flight of stairs to a very small room which was in fact the basement. It must have measured about 14 feet by 10 feet. It was only illuminated by a number of candles and the congregation consisted of 9 other people who were also black. What immediately affected us both was the truly peaceful and tranquil atmosphere in this little room. It was truly beautiful and so rare to find.

We enjoyed a very good service there and everyone received a message from Clive. After the service one of the people there introduced themselves to us and he was the Bishop of the local Pentecostal church. He was quite overwhelmed with the service.

On one occasion we arrived for a Sunday service at a church in Slough which had just had its AGM. Regrettably Spiritualism and AGMs do not seem to go together well in many churches and often the atmosphere after such a meeting can be heavily polluted. People seem to hold onto their gripes and grudges and them let them all out at the AGM. We were shown into the mediums room by the new President, someone we had not met before and did not warm to and when we enquired what had happened to the previous one we were told "Oh we got rid of him at the AGM." With that he left us.

Not a very spiritual response. Clive told me that it was clear that there had been some "fun and games here". A few minutes later the President returned to tell us that he would be chairing and another lady would be giving a reading and that all four of us would be going onto the rostrum. The rostrum however was only small and was already overcrowded with three of us, let alone four. He introduced the lady to us who was in a complete nervous and dishevelled state and clearly not ready to go onto a rostrum and was behaving very erratically mumbling away to herself and twitching uncontrollably. The president was totally oblivious to this situation and when Clive seeing this asked him discreetly if the lady was fit to go on the rostrum he was met with an emphatic "Of course!"

Well the service duly started and the pompous president did a very good job of patronising the congregation within minutes. Both Clive and I felt very uncomfortable with the developing situation and it did not auger well for a good service. The final straw came when the lady attempted to give the reading and just could not do it at all and the service just disintegrated into a complete farce. At this point we made our excuses and left. However the majority of the churches we have served were run much better and we have enjoyed some truly great times.

Commitment and dedication to spirit and churches is vitally important. Indeed in over 50 years of working for spirit Clive has only let down two churches. On both occasions it has, sadly, been my fault as my car broke down on the motorway. Still it is a pretty good track record and is in sharp contrast with some mediums who let down churches often and with very feeble reasons.

7

HEALING

One of the first things I decided to try out was all this "nonsense" about the healing gift that several mediums told me I had. Now in the office was the MD's secretary Margaret and one day when I came in I noticed that she had one of those foam collars around her neck. I asked why she was wearing it and she told me that she was playing judo with her son the previous night and he had flung her over his shoulder and the net result was that she had jarred her neck badly. Right I thought, I will try this healing thing tonight when I get home. So that night I pictured Margaret in my mind and asked spirit to use me as best they could and sent out healing thoughts to Margaret.

The following morning when I arrived at the office I walk past Margaret and noticed, with a little surprise, that she was not wearing the collar. I stopped and asked her why she was not wearing it and she said "Oh it felt better this morning so I have left it off". Hmm, I thought, must be pure coincidence. But over time I have been very fortunate to have experienced many such "coincidences".

However there have been times when I have felt very disillusioned with my healing work. Now I would like everyone that I practice healing on to immediately feel the benefit, a kind of instant healing. Sometimes when I give healing I do not feel anything at all, no warmth, coldness, tingling etc just nothing at all. In these situations I would wonder if spirit were with me at all and was I just standing there being totally inadequate.

I was going through a period like this and feeling quiet sorry for myself and happened to visit my mother. At that time she had a visitor staying a few days who was an elderly polish lady who I called auntie and knew me from a small boy. We had eaten our supper and my mother had to go out for a while so we were left alone to chat. The subject of spiritualism and in particular healing came up and I mentioned that I did do healing.

My aunt immediately asked me if I would give here healing. I was really quiet reluctant as I felt so inadequate and as I was going through this spell of "doubt". But I did feel that you should never refuse a request and so I agreed. We both went into the lounge and I sat her on a chair and explained that I would put my hands on her shoulders and say a prayer asking for my healing guides to draw close and use me as best as they could. Then I would place my hands lightly on various parts of her body and she may or may not feel anything but regardless she would feel the benefit of healing.

So I put my hands on her shoulders. She sat very still. I then opened with a quiet prayer and asked for my healing guides to draw clo... I had not even finished asking when to my surprise my aunt started to tremble in her seat. I continued with my prayer and her trembling became more vibrant. I carried out my healing in my usual way and placed my hands lightly on various parts of her body. Her legs had now started trembling up and down such that the soles of her shoes were bouncing on the floor, her jaw was chattering and I could hear her teeth banging against each other.

I started to get very concerned because here was an elderly lady in her 80s and I felt that this healing could not possibly do her any good at all, on the contrary it might do the complete opposite, but I persevered. I then came back to her shoulders and rested my hands on them as I was finishing the healing. She continued to tremble. I then sent out a silent prayer to my healing guides and asked them to stop as I had finished. Again before I had completed my prayer she was already beginning to stop trembling and by the time I had finished the prayer she had stopped completely. It was just as if someone was turning off a tap.

I looked at her in a rather concerned way and asked how she felt. She told me that she felt fine and had never experienced anything like that. Her only concern was, that with her jaw chattering so much, she thought her false teeth might have fallen out.

So another lesson learnt for me which was if you ask help from spirit you will receive it regardless of whether you feel any sensations or not.

Over the years I have been very fortunate to have had some very humbling experiences where patients have felt immediate relief from certain symptoms. I just wish there had been many more but, once again, you do your part and allow spirit to do theirs.

8

BEDFORD

We continued our work and did discuss from time to time how good it would be to live out in the peace and quite of the country surrounded by fields. This after time began to become a hotter topic for us. Clive had always dreamed of living in the country and running a boarding kennels as well as breeding his Pekingese dogs which he showed. He had done very well in the breed and had shown at Cruffs on a number of occasions.

After some considerable thought and discussion we decided to sell our respective homes and pool the money to buy a kennels somewhere in the country. Clive would run the kennels and I would continue in the computer business but be able to help Clive in the evenings and at weekends as necessary. The location had to be ideally no more than an hours drive to my office which was at Maple X, Rickmansworth, Herts.

We visited a number of establishments but none were suitable and then we got a specification for a place outside of Bedford near the village of Stagsden. It looked a good possibility so we decided to arrange a viewing. We went to view on a Sunday morning and had some difficulty finding it as it was down an isolated country lane. But find it we did and as we drove into the drive Clive immediately said "this is it, I'm home".

We were shown around the property, by a lady, which comprised some 2 acres with several outbuildings. It had two cattery blocks and could board up to 50 cats and a single kennel block which housed 6 dog pens. The original part of the house dated back over 200 years and it had had an extension of a kitchen and bathroom. A double garage had also been converted into some additional rooms.

Following our tour we were both smitten with the property and were about to make an offer when she said "there is just one thing I should tell you and that is that it is already sold". Clive could hardly contain himself but did somehow manage. In fact it had not been sold but they had received an offer which they accepted and thing were moving forward. I did tell her that if anything should happened with the sale would she please give me a ring. We left the property feeling dejected although I remained optimistic. If we were meant to have it then we would.

Some weeks later I was in my flat getting ready to go out and pick Clive up when the phone rang. The sale had fallen through, we were back in the running and a few months later on 17th July 1985 we moved into Park Farm.

I had taken two weeks holiday to coincide with the move as there was much to be done. However a week after the move my sales director rang me at home and asked if we could meet and "have a chat" the following day. This could mean anything and clearly was not a good sign. I had a very worrying 24 hours. The next day we met in a hotel just off junction 8 on the M1 motorway. As I entered the hotel I had feelings of trepidation as I just knew that the news would not be good. I was right. He told me that at the end of the month the office at Maple X would be closed down and I would then be based in Brighton. Now Maple X was 45 miles from Park Farm while the Brighton office was 125 miles away.

I was devastated as was Clive when I told him. We had just moved into our new home and it now looked as if everything was about to fall apart. However we are both very positive people and remained so, although the outlook was in reality apparently bleak. When I returned to the office, a number of meetings and some heavy negotiation took place over a few days, with the net result being that I and my sales team would now be based from our respective homes. Success! But for how long?

My business work would take me all over the country and there would be times when I was away overnight. On one of these trips Clive decided to visit the local spiritualist church in Bedford where we had not been before. When he arrived he was greeted warmly by a lady at the door and they had a general chat before he sat down. Shortly afterwards another lady sat next to him and they too started chatting. The time came for the service to start but only the chairman went onto the platform and announced that the booked medium had not arrived. He asked if there was a medium in the congregation. Clive had said nothing to anybody about him being a working medium as he is always reluctant to push himself forward, but the lady next to him turned to him and said "you are a medium aren't you?" Clive confirmed that he was and the net result was he took the service which went down very well.

Following the success of that night the word quickly spread and we started to receive bookings from churches in the area.

We soon settled into a routine which was that Clive worked in the cattery starting at 7.00am and when I had no appointments and was working at home I would join him at about 7.30am. We would be finished by 9.00am so I would go into my office and Clive would see to customers for the cattery. In the evenings and weekends we would be out serving churches who had booked us.

This went on for about a year when there were some more changes in the office with the net result that I now would, after all, be based in Brighton. So our routine changed and I would now have to leave Park Farm on a Monday morning at 5.45am drive down the M1, onto the M25 and then down the M23 to Brighton. I would stop a few miles short of the office at a Little Chef for "an early starter breakfast" and then be sat at my desk before 9.00am. Clearly this journey of 125 miles each way was not for a daily commute so I had to find some sort of digs in Brighton. I managed to find a small room in a flat where the landlady was also resident. The contrast from home and my little bed-sit was extreme. At home we had a large house with all mod cons while the bed-sit had one electric ring for cooking which I used to good effect for my "boil in the bag" meals. For the next 7 years there was not a working week when I slept at home each night.

I found my contrasting lifestyle quiet funny because for example on a Sunday morning we would be in the cattery cleaning out upto 50 litter trays and preparing 50 dinners. In the evening we would be taking a Sunday service and on the Monday I could be doing a Board presentation to a large corporation extolling the virtues of my companies computer systems.

I also found being a salesman and also a spiritualist

could be a contrasting combination. I knew for example that most of my competitors would "stretch wildly" the truth and sometimes downright lie about their respective products and their capabilities all to the detriment of ours. I decided that I would always be honest in what our company could or could not do. This methodology I know lost me some business but I also know it gained me a lot more because my integrity was not compromised. Once my customers realised this then I would get excellent recommendations and repeat business.

Of course from time to time things did go wrong with my or my colleagues clients and occasionally customers would become almost hysterical when their computer systems failed and the business ground to a virtual halt. Some heavy-duty meetings with then took place. These I found a challenge and by listening, without interruption, to them sometimes pouring out their frustration and verbal ranting did make them feel better. Prior to such meetings however I would bring some spiritual knowledge to bear by sending out healing thoughts to all that were to be present at the meeting and also asked for spirit to help me in what I did and said.

The net result was that I gained a reputation in the company that if anyone had a problem customer they would say "get Wojtek involved because meetings always go better when he is present." Indeed some customers, at the end of such meetings, would apologise to me for speaking out so bluntly at the beginning. I knew though that it was my friends in spirit who made the meetings easier.

Some more years went by and then we were taken over by a new company and we had a new board of directors. Things stayed the same for me (more or less) but we all felt a bit under the microscope and knew more changes were inevitable. All our history with our original employer was virtually washed away and we had to start afresh.

The changes did come but they effected me in a good way as I was now to be based in the Rugby office (40 miles North from Park Farm) which was about an hours drive from home. This now meant that I could sleep at home every night and have decent meals...success!

9

PARK FARM GATHERINGS

Sometimes we would serve churches and do a "Special" which quiet often was a charity event where we took no fee and all proceeds went to a particular charity. We decided that we would like to do something spiritual ourselves at Park Farm for a charity. Shortly afterwards we became aware of Botton Village (www. camphill.org.uk) which was a village where mentally handicapped people of varying ages and abilities lived with different families in houses dotted around the locality. The "Villagers" as they are called all had jobs to do be it working in the dairy, gardens, bakery etc.

This charity appealed to us so we set about holding Park Farm Gatherings and would try to hold one every month or so. Our gatherings consisted of us inviting about 18-20 people from a spiritualist church to our home. They would arrive by 1 pm and have a cup of tea and generally settle, as some would have travelled over 50 miles to get to us. We would then have a trance session where Clive would allow his Chinese guide Woo Wang to take control and speak to the people for a short while and then invite questions. The questions that were asked could be on any topic and each questioner had the opportunity to ask any supplementary points to what had been given. The trance lasted for about

90 minutes at which point we broke for lunch. In the summer this consisted of a cold buffet with salmon, different varieties of quiches, sausage rolls, salads etc, in the winter it was a hot meal of a meat/veg pie and three veg. This was followed by a trifle or fruit pie and custard and tea/coffee.

We then resumed the meeting with an hour of clairvoyance given by Clive which was followed by Spiritual Healing given by myself and several others. The healing sessions were a very peaceful part of the day where the atmosphere within our sanctuary changed to a much more tranquil vibration and the heat generated in the room was very noticeable. Many would comment on how uplifting they felt that this part of the day was for them. After the healing was completed the gathering was closed and it was back to the kitchen for tea/coffee and home made cakes and plenty of chatting.

When we organised these meetings we decide that we would not charge but have a "free-will offering plate" and people would put in what they felt was appropriate. This way we felt that those who may be financially strapped could still come to our meetings. From the money donated we would take out just the cost of the food and the balance we would send to Botton Village. I would receive a letter of thanks from Botton with the amount donated and would then forward a copy to the church which visited us so that they could see exactly how much was raised.

We really enjoyed running these gatherings as to see the joy and happiness that it brought to the people who visited was very heart warming. It was a lot of hard work as we started preparations the week before and made full use of the freezers. The day of the event was rather frantic because we had the cattery to see to first of all and then get ourselves and everything ready for our visitors. Fortunately we did have a few volunteer helpers which helped the day go much smoother.

We continued with our gatherings for a number of years and were able to donate a substantial amount during this time to Botton Village. Most of the time our visitors were generous and we had a sum of money to send on but there were a few occasions were regrettably the money donated did not even cover the cost of the food. This was very disappointing and upsetting particularly as out visitors were supposed to be "spiritualists".

However on one occasion we had a group from Japan. They were in the UK for a few weeks and were visiting various spiritualist centres etc. Upon arrival at our home the group leader gave Clive an envelope from one of the party who could not come but nonetheless wanted to make a donation. Clive opened the envelope and inside was £1,000. The Japanese group really enjoyed their day with us and were very appreciative of what we had laid on for them. Before leaving the group leader invited us out to Japan to work there and we made several trips over the next few years. When they left we went over to the donations plate and it was full of £50 notes. As a result we were able to make the biggest ever donation to Botton Village.

10

WORKING OVERSEAS

While we lived at Park Farm we had a phone enquiry via The London Spiritualist Mission in London, which we served, that a lady (Tanmayo) from Germany was looking for mediums for a centre that she had just started. Before she would book any English mediums she wanted to assess their abilities, which is a very reasonable request. So one Saturday we drove down to her hotel in London and Clive gave her a sitting with her son present. After the sitting she immediately made a booking and both Clive and I went to Munich in Germany the following year to carry our public clairvoyant demonstrations, private sittings, a seminar and spiritual healing. It was hard work with long hours especially for Clive as he had to have an interpreter which made each message in effect twice as long.

Interestingly although Clive has no knowledge of the German language he told the interpreter to translate exactly what he said without making any changes. A couple of times during the clairvoyant demonstrations the interpreter said something in German to the recipient of the message and Clive immediately pounced on her before she had even finished speaking and said "you are not translating exactly what I am saying!" and he was always correct. We worked in Germany several times.

On another occasion we had finished the Sunday evening service at The London Spiritual Mission and had gone into the library for tea and to mingle with the congregation. A lady (Sara) approached us who was on holiday from America where she lived in Santa Monica just outside of Los Angeles. She said if we were ever going to be in the States she would be able to arrange a few meetings. Strangely at this time there was a competition running in the office which was if we sold three computer systems of a particular type then we would be rewarded by a paid visit to the American plant where the computers were manufactured. We could then add on our holiday.

Fortunately I was successful in selling the required number of systems and in November 1987 we arrived at San Francisco International Airport. We stayed in the Sheraton Hotel on Fisherman's Wharf. San Francisco was great! A few days later we drove down the Pacific Coast Highway to Santa Monica and arranged to met up with Sara who had made some bookings for us.

We arrived at Sara's mobile home and as she carried out spiritual healing she had a couch laid out in her lounge and was waiting for a few patients to arrive. She asked us if we could just wait a little while and then she would be free. The patients arrived shortly afterwards and after a brief chat the first one laid down on the couch. Sara then proceeded to give her healing by placing her hands on various parts of her body as she walked around the couch. Then all of a sudden we heard a "bodily wind noise" emanate from Sara. Clive and I being polite just ignored it. But shortly after it happened again but this time much louder and with more gusto. This continued time after time during the whole healing session. Bizarre. The next patient got on the couch and the same procedure was followed by Sara and once again she let rip with a continuing stream of flatulent sounds which went up and down the scale for noise and duration.

We could not believe what was going on particularly as the patients seemed completely un-phased by her actions. After the patients left we could not help ourselves but ask Sara why she was making all these flatulent noise all the time that she was healing. She said that it was her method of clearing the patients impurities. We found this a very unconvincing answer because at the very least if this was the case then surely it should have been the patient who made these noises and not Sara.

But the interesting and most important point here is that these patients, that came to her, did tell her that they felt better after a healing session. So again it is the end result that is important and not perhaps the methodology.

We served a number of churches and groups in Los Angeles as well as one in San Diego. In between these we managed to go site seeing and visited Disneyland which we found a very magical experience. It was great to see the young children bouncing into the theme park in the morning full of excitement and anticipation. Which was in sharp contrast to the evening when they slowly trudged out exhausted and satisfied, adorned with various Mickey Mouse memorabilia. We too were no different. A few days later we also managed to visit Universal Studios which was another fun experience.

In October 1996 we went on our first trip to Japan following the invitation we received at Park Farm when the Japanese group visited our home. We found Japan beautiful and the people very friendly and warm. We carried out various engagements of clairvoyance, trance, healing and a seminar. Our hosts looked after us very well and we were able to experience and enjoy several different traditional Japanese restaurants.

One amusing incident was when we had just been met at the airport and taken for lunch. Clive informed our host that he was a vegetarian so could he order something appropriate. This he acknowledged to do. However several minutes later a large steamy bowl arrived and is put in front of Clive who peered into it inquisitively with ever bulging eyes and then started to turn quiet pale. What he sees is some strange flat like "creatures" wriggling about on top of the steaming vegetables.

He enquired hesitantly what these "creatures" were to which all the locals collapsed in hysterical laughter. The "creatures" were in fact very thin slivers of dried tuna fish which once placed on the hot food started to curl up and twist about.

11

FORGIVENESS

Knowing of the extreme mental cruelty Clive went through at the hands of his father made it impossible for me to have any good thoughts about this man even though he had passed into spirit in 1969. Yet as I travelled on my spiritual journey I had learnt many things and I hope continue to do so. Many years ago there were certain people that I hated and all my thoughts towards them were of this tenure. While I had learnt not to hate anybody now, regardless of who they were or what they had done, because this was a negative way to be. Instead if there was someone I just could not stand I would send out zero thoughts to them. I at least had learnt the old adage of "as you sow, so shall you reap".

In time I learnt that this too was not helpful and what I should do instead, to such individuals, is swamp them in thoughts of Love, Peace and Harmony. This would help the condition not only for them but also for me. I did find this very difficult and initially virtually sent out such thoughts "through gritted teeth" even though deep down I knew that this was not the correct thing to do.

I recall in the office that following a take-over I had a new boss. Someone whom I and my colleagues, found very abrasive, aggressive, inconsiderate and unreasonable. From our first meeting we just did not "gel" together at all. To me he was like a dark cloud strutting the office ready to explode for any reason be it justified or not. This was not a good omen for the future and did prey on my mind.

After some difficult days and meetings with him I decide to change my tact with this individual and now decided that I would swamp him in thoughts of Love, Peace and Harmony. This I did each night and whenever I went to see him. Within a very few weeks of me changing my attitude towards him and sending out these positive thoughts, his attitude towards me changed for the better. Success! So we had some positive progress as a result of me changing my attitude for the better. We never became the best of buddies but did get on better.

Now bearing this in mind I still remained a hypocrite when it came to Clive's dad because I just could not, would not, understand or forgive the treatment he showed to his son which in my mind was very wicked, cruel and sadistic. Whenever I would think of the horrible things he subjected, a very young, Clive to made me furious with anger.

But, in the churches on Sunday we would recite the Lord's Prayer and one passage kept sticking in my mind:-

"forgive us our trespasses as we
forgive those that trespass against us"

In other words I regularly asked for forgiveness for the wrong things that I had done and also asked for people who had done me a wrong to be forgiven also. But how on earth could I forgive Clive's father for the terrible cruel and wicked things he had done to his own son. I was torn and angry because I just could not (or perhaps would not) reconcile these two things. Various thoughts came into my head like, "judge not lest you be judged" or "an eye for an eye and a tooth for a tooth", and then "turn the other cheek".

What was I to make of all of this when it came to Clive's dad. I wrestled with this for quiet some time and I guess battled with my physical thoughts which were on the vibration of "I'd like to strangle the bast**d!" to my spiritual side which said "you must forgive". So this was one of those difficult lessons that comes our way from time to time and nobody to help resolve this dichotomy except me.

After some time of mulling this over I eventually came to a decision. I decided that I would forgive but not forget. Why forgive? Well who was I to judge him. I do not know what drove him to do the things that he did. Was he a vicious bully? Did he have a mental problem? Did he blame Clive, subconsciously, for his wife's death? Etc etc.

So one day when the house was empty I sat down in the conservatory. It was a pleasantly warm day with the sun breaking through the thin clouds and I could hear the birds singing in the garden as they flew around the bird table. I put a soothing and relaxing tape into my "ghetto blaster" and pressed play.

I sat back and sunk into a cane garden seat, closed my eyes and sent out a prayer. In essence I sent out my thoughts to the world of spirit to help and assist me at this time. I asked for the spirit of Clive's dad to draw close. In my mind I spoke to him and told him that while I did not understand his actions to Clive I did now forgive him for those same actions. In other words I released him from my negativity towards him.

My thoughts continued for a little while in this manner and then I closed with a short prayer and slowly opened my eyes.

I felt very emotional and little odd afterwards it was as if a great big weight had been lifted from my shoulders. I somehow felt "free". I said nothing to Clive about this experience when he returned home.

The following Sunday we had a free day and decided to go to Wigan for the Sunday service. We did not know who the medium was so it was potluck who we got. When we arrived there we looked on the notice board to see who the medium was and were a little disappointed as we had seen this particular lady work before, in another church and felt that at that service she left a lot to be desired in her clairvoyance.

The service started and we now come to the clairvoyant part. Straight away she came to Clive and said that she had his father with her. She said that his father had come specifically to say "sorry" for the way he had treated Clive and that he was very proud of him and the work he had done and continues to do for spirit. He asked for Clive's forgiveness which Clive readily gave. This was a unique message because Clive had never had a message from his father before. I believe that this was all made possible as a result of the earlier occurrence in the conservatory some days earlier.

The lesson that I learnt here was that in forgiving Clive's dad not only did I set him free to progress spiritually but at the same time I set myself free of that negative condition too, which also enabled me to take a few more spiritual steps. Clive also benefited as it was the first time his father had apologised to him and they now enjoy a better relationship than before.

So the lesson here is that if you have someone

around you, that has in your view "wronged you", then perhaps it is time to let this condition go. To forgive not necessarily forget and in so doing free yourself of this negative imposition upon yourself that you allow to continue. I know and understand that this can be very difficult to do but the alternative is to allow the condition to go on and on and fester, which in turn makes life more difficult for all concerned.

12

HONOURABLE WOO WANG

I have made reference to Woo Wang several times in this book so it is right and proper that I tell you something more about this individual and the work he has and continues to do through Clive.

When Clive was still a small boy he would on occasion, while in bed, see standing at the foot of his bed a figure of an old man with long and colourful silk embroidered robes that went to the floor. He was yellowish in colour and gaunt looking with a long thin grey beard, when he smiled he showed that he only had one tooth left in the front of his gums. On his head he wore a small hat. Clive was not frightened of this individual, it was more that he was just puzzled by him. This Chinese man would also appear at other times in other places and sometimes outside of the home. He did not speak but would just look and smile.

When Clive started attending the circle run by Nan Cowling there would, as part of the meeting, be a time where everyone sat quietly to see if spirit would come. This could be in the sense of people receiving information which they would subsequently pass on to the other sitters or it could be that someone becomes entranced and spoke to the group.

On the first occasion that Clive sat in the circle and

the group went into the "quiet" he soon became aware of someone standing beside him. This he recognised as the spirit of Woo Wang. It was a strange sensation because as Woo Wang moved his mouth so the spoken words came out of Clive's mouth. While the others in the circle found what was being said interesting Clive found it to be an unpleasant experience. He therefore said, in his thoughts to Woo Wang, that he did not want to work in this way but rather be fully entranced. Ever since that day this has been how Woo Wang has worked with Clive.

We do know quiet a lot about Woo Wang from questions that have been put to him over the years. He tells us that he was of high birth and was on the earth plane at the time that the Great Wall of China was being built. He was elevated to Marshall King of China and had many Palaces. But he was an extremely cruel man and for example when he was carried through the streets in a chair his people had to fall to the ground with bowed heads. If anyone looked up at him then their head would be completely severed.

He had many wives and people would also bring their daughters to him at the palace so that he would look after them. He tells us that he had a wife for every day of the year but did not "use" them all. Since his Chinese incarnation he has reincarnated many times. Sometimes as a man and sometimes as a woman. Now he always shows himself in his Chinese incarnation as this was the life where he learnt the most.

It was at the latter part of his life when his number one wife passed away and he was truly distraught. He went for a walk in his gardens and sat by a pool and looked into the water and there, reflected in the water he saw his wife who spoke to him and pointed out the wickedness of his ways. It was then that Woo Wang repented for his actions and started his long road to greater spirituality. That road still continues.

Woo Wang tells us that he is on the seventh plane of learning and when Clive passes into the world of spirit then he will progress onto the eighth plane. Once there he will no longer come back to the earth plane, as a Spirit Guide and entrance someone. But he would become a guide to a guide that will link with the earth plane in a more direct way which could be through trance.

When Clive started to work for spirit at the age of 17 and demonstrate his gift of clairvoyance he was still very shy and nervous. He therefore decided that the only way to work for spirit would be to allow Woo Wang to entrance him and take full control. For many years now, when demonstrating, Clive would therefore go into a deep trance state and Woo Wang would take full control of all of Clive's faculties. At these times Clive's spirit would in effect leave his physical body and stand to one side although still be linked to it by the silver etheric cord.

Once the meeting was over Clive would come back but he had no awareness at all of anything that had transpired. After a few years Clive started to demonstrate clairvoyance in churches without going into trance. The trance work was then used for private groups and when churches or others wished to have a question and answer session.

Theses question and answer sessions proved to be popular as members of the congregation were able to ask any question on any topic. Once Woo Wang had given his answer he would always ask if they wanted to ask any supplementary questions. Occasionally some would and a good debate was had. Since I became involved I decided to tape all the trance meetings and now have several cases full of tapes going back many years.

Over the years Woo Wang has been quizzed by various scholars and professors from various educational establishments. Some would be trying to understand trance, some wanted information about life in China at the time Woo Wang was there. Others were just curious and tried to asked what they felt were trick questions. Woo Wang always came out with "flying colours" and much praise.

One very important characteristic with Woo Wang that I have noticed is that when ever he is asked a question he immediately and without hesitation comes back with an answer. It just flows. He does not require any thinking time before he delivers a response. Indeed that is as it should be because he is highly evolved, if it were not so then there would be much hesitation and "ums and errs" before and during the response.

Naturally as I was now always present at theses trance sessions I got to know Woo Wang more than anyone else. On quiet a few occasions when we had some free evenings Clive would come over to my flat and we would "do Woo Wang". So I had a personal and private opportunity to talk and listen to Woo Wang. These sessions were not for me just to have survival evidence instead they were more like I suppose a father son situation where I would ask him various questions. These could be about material work, my relationship with Clive, our church work etc. We would just chat about all sorts of things. Once we moved to Bedford these all but ceased.

These sessions were truly great times, full of laughter, intrigue and sometimes tears, which I guess I only now fully appreciate. It was also at these times that once Woo Wang had left that two spirit children would come and speak. Namely Richard and Johnny. More about them later.

Woo Wang continues to impact both our lives as he is around us often and influences us in many things that we do. He has and is an inspiration to us both and remains our spiritual rock.

13

RESCUE WORK

This term is quite often heard within the Spiritualist movement and does have a number of definitions. Ours is, that where a spirit has left the physical body but does not understand that this is the case then it is referred to as "earth bound". The spirit then has to be "rescued" that is to say to make it aware of what has happened and allow it to fully return back into the world of spirit.

In our work visiting many churches we came across groups of people who had a special "rescue circle" whose whole purpose was to gather together and rescue spirits that were earth bound. Clive has always thought that this is really quiet unnecessary because surely those that are already in the world of spirit, without a physical body, are far better equipped to help, than people on the earth plane, who do still have a physical body. I could see the logic in this and it did make perfect sense to me as well. But...

Clive and I started to sit together on a regular basis in our own circle, just the two of us. We did not seek to get involved with rescue work but just to sit quietly and meditate. One of us would open in a prayer and then Clive would typically give a theme for a meditation and we would sit in the quiet for a little while, usually 20 to 30 minutes. This would be a time where we could mutually relax and tune into spirit.

We had been doing this for a few weeks when on one particular evening, while we were meditating, I became aware of Clive fidgeting in his chair and making some muffled sounds. I opened my eyes and looked over at him. He was still sitting in his chair with his eyes closed but I felt that he had been taken over by a spirit. I was not concerned because I had seen Clive in trance on many occasions with Woo Wang so thought that this might be him coming through or, to my logic, a new and similarly evolved guide.

However, when I said "hello" I was greeted by a rough Liverpudlian male voice who told me in quiet an eloquent but aggressive tone to "f**k off!" This took be aback some-what and threw me for a short while as I was not used to hearing such language from spirit. I was not sure what to expect next so decided to proceed very cautiously. To my mind here was a spirit which had entranced Clive so I had to find out why and help as much as I could.

I asked him if he was alright and he just told me to leave him alone. I had now assumed that this was one of these earth bound spirits which needed to be "rescued". So I gently questioned him about what had happened to him recently to find out how I could help him most. After some time I began to gain his confidence. I found out that he had gone to a football match to watch Liverpool play and on the way out of the Anfield ground he had got into a fight and was stabbed. He did make it home and his mother started to fuss about as she could clearly see he had been in a fight as there was blood all down his front. He told her to "go away and leave me alone, don't call the busies". This she eventually and reluctantly did and he lay down on his bed in his room.

I asked him what happened next. He said he did not know but things were now "different". I explained to him that as a result of his injuries his body had died but he, that is to say his spirit, was very much alive. I told him that Clive had allowed his spirit to leave his own body and that he had now allowed him to enter. I carried on talking to him and reassuring him that all was well and that he was not dead but very much alive but in the world of spirit. He found this difficult to take in but as he knew that he had felt "different" then perhaps I was right. We carried on chatting and I asked him if Liverpool won the match. He told me no and that "they played as if they had been fed on marmalade."

I then asked him if anyone had brought him to Clive and he told me that a young Victorian girl called Lydia had done so. Yes the very same girl that works with Clive during clairvoyance.

Now we come to one of the key aspects of rescue work and why we on the earth plain, in physical bodies are, depending on the circumstances, better equipped to help these "lost souls". When it was time to close our circle I had to explain that it was time for him to go and leave Clive's body. It would be a bit like dying again except that this time he will know that he still lives but only in the spirit sense. I told him to go with Lydia and she would help him. With that he drifted away and Clive drifted back, totally unaware that anything had happened.

These encounters with "lost souls" continued to occur for a number of months. Some were very tragic and sad but occasionally the conversation and misunderstandings between us were hilarious. There were a few incidents which were also very difficult where the "lost soul" did not want to leave Clive and stayed for upto two hours threatening me with all sorts if they could not stay.

One such case was a lady that came who was from the East end of London and clearly was a "working girl". Her name was Rose. I was being very polite to her and trying to fathom how best to help her, when she started to proposition me and was most annoyed when I did not respond positively. She then started to call me all sorts of names which started from being a prude and escalated to others which are not at all suitable to be added here.

From our conversation it was obvious that she was totally unaware that she had passed into the world of spirit. I had to very gently try to explain that she had in fact passed over but she would have none of it and started to get more and more agitated and aggressive towards me. At one point she grabbed a vase off a table and tried to bash me with it. Fortunately she missed.

I was racking my brains to find out what I could do or say that would convince her that she was indeed in spirit. I had already explained that she had taken control of Clive and was using his body but she would have none of it and went off on another rant. Then I had a brainwave and said to her "OK then. Touch your breasts". With that she placed her hands on her chest and then WWIII erupted. She went potty "where are they, where are they, what's happened, what have you done?" I said "now touch your hair" and this time her hands went to her head and ruffled Clive's hair. "This is not my hair! What's happening?"

Slowly I managed to explain and convince her that she was indeed in the world of spirit and very reluctantly she seemed to accept this and eventually, after over two hours of battling, she left Clive. Both Clive and I were exhausted.

I always tape recorded these encounters so do now have a box full of tapes which documents all our experiences.

Two very notable "rescues" concerned a little boy called Johnny who was four and a half and also Richard who was fourteen. These two have featured very much in our lives since. Johnny is featured in the next chapter and Richard's story is at the Appendix. Both of them are around us all the time and we are very much aware of their presence and in Richard's case his mischief making. Both of them have spoken through Clive at a number of churches when we have had a question and answer session with Woo Wang. Once the questions are over quite often they would come through and speak for a little while. They would both have the audience roaring with laughter but for very different reasons.

14

THE KIDS!

Clive and I both love children and it is, most of the time, a joy to be in their company particularly when they are well behaved. Obviously we shall never have our own children in the traditional sense but Spirit Children is another matter.

Back in 1952 Clive was working in a shoe shop and had Wednesdays afternoons off as it was half-day closing. He had gone home and was feeling a bit unwell with a sore throat and lay down on the couch in his lounge. He closed his eyes and was dozing when he started to hear a child's laughter. He opened his eyes and there standing at the end of the couch was a young girl dressed in Victorian clothes. She stayed for a little while and then left.

A few days later while Clive was cleaning the house he went into the lounge and there standing underneath a chandelier was this same Victorian girl again. This time however she had a sad expression and kept looking up at the chandelier. Clive looked up at the chandelier too and saw that it actually was very dirty and in need of a good clean. Several days later he cleaned it thoroughly and it truly sparkled. It was at its best when the sunlight caught the droplets and reflected rainbow colours filled the room. A few days later he again goes into the lounge and the Victorian girls is standing underneath the chandelier but this time she looks up at it and smiles.

This young girl is Lydia who is twelve and a half and always shows herself to Clive dressed in the clothes of the period. She went into the world of Spirit, while Queen Victoria still reigned, with diphtheria.

The chandelier mentioned is actually made up of a number of pieces from different chandeliers and we subsequently found out that some of the pieces were from a chandelier that was in one of the homes where Lydia lived.

At this time in Clive's work for spirit, when he demonstrated in the churches he would always allow his Chinese Guide Woo Wang to come through and give the clairvoyance while old Harry would give the address. Clive had been booked to do a Special in Ealing at a church in Bakers Lane. On the evening that they arrived they found that the church was packed with only standing room left. When it came to the time for clairvoyance Clive, as always sat down, closed his eyes and asked Woo Wang to take control and do the demonstration. But on this particular night when Clive asked for Woo Wang absolutely nothing happened, he could still feel that he was very much conscious of all his surroundings and was unable to go into trance. He tried again, all the congregation were looking at him in eager anticipation but again nothing happened. Oh no he thought, what happens now. So he stood up and said "ladies and gentleman I am very sorry but nothing seems to be happening to night......" and then all of a sudden right at the back of the room he saw Lydia and she was pointing at a gentleman next to her.

Clive was confused and puzzled but said to this

particular gentleman "Hello, God Bless you". He had no idea what he was going to say next but as soon as the man responded and Clive heard his voice the clairvoyance started to flow. More importantly it was all understood. When he had no more to give he looked around the church and there was Lydia again pointing to somebody else and Clive spoke to them. This procedure was carried on through out the evening and all to great success.

Since that time right to the present, when Clive demonstrates Clairvoyance, it is Lydia who chooses the people who are to receive the messages.

The years rolled by and we now come to the 1980s. It is during the times when we encountered the "Rescue" situations that the next spirit child was brought to us. This was Johnny who was a four and a half year old boy who passed in rather tragic circumstances. I have reproduced below an article published in 1993 which gives you the full background to this sad situation.

"This story starts back in 1981 and happened while I was sitting in a circle with trance medium Clive Daniels, just the two of us. It was during a meditation that I became aware and also heard the whimpering of what appeared to be a young child. I opened my eyes and looked at Clive and saw that he had been entranced by a Spirit. I said, "Hello, God Bless you" and this very sad and tearful voice responded "I'm hungry, I want my mummy, the bed is messy, I'm frightened".

I had some experience of these situations as they had happened in the past. I knew that this little boy had obviously passed into the world of Spirit but had not realised that he had left the earthly conditions behind. I was very upset because how could I explain to this poor child that he was now free of those material conditions.

I could not tell him that he had died or passed over as I felt that this would only frighten him more. After all he did tell me that he was only four and a half years old and his name was Johnny.

I felt so inadequate. I did however tell this little boy to speak to Lydia (she is a Spirit child that would bring these lost souls to speak through Clive) and she would take him to meet his mummy and give him some food. The child tearfully and obviously very frightened left.

I was greatly saddened by this experience as I felt that I had not been of any real help at all. This sadness stayed with me until about a week later when Clive was giving a group trance sitting. On these occasions he would allow his Chinese guide Woo Wang to talk through him to the sitters. At the end of the sittings Woo Wang turned to me and told me that little "Johnny Boy" was much better now. He had been to see his mother, had been well fed and had had a jolly good bath. Woo Wang further explained that Johnny was born outside of marriage and was being taken care of by his mother only. However his mother was sub-normal and did not realise that Johnny was a fast growing boy or indeed how to look after him properly. One day she put Johnny to bed, locked the bedroom door and left. Several weeks later she returned and of course Johnny had passed.

A week or so later Clive and I were again sitting in our circle and little Johnny came and spoke through Clive to me. He very shyly said "thank you for helping me" and then very hesitantly asked, "will..., will you be my Daddy, I never had one before". Naturally I said yes but a little bewildered, as I did not know what a Daddy to a Spirit boy would really entail.

Well over the weeks, months and years Johnny and

I have developed what I can only describe as a normal Father Son relationship. Johnny is as real to me as any physical Son is to anybody else.

I remember an amusing incident at the beginning of our relationship. I asked Johnny, who at that time was four and half years old, the date of his birthday. He immediately responded "November 51!" I told him that November did not have 51 days but Johnny was very insistent. The 51 I feel may relate to 1951. So I settled on the 15th as being the birthday date. I asked Johnny what he would like for his birthday and without hesitation he said "a chopper bike".

I discussed this present with Clive afterwards and said we have a real problem here because how on earth can we give a Spirit child a present. Clive looked at the ceiling with that "why am I surrounded with fools" expression and informed me that it really was quiet simple. All we had to do is picture the bike in our minds and send it to Johnny in our thoughts on his birthday.

Now this was straight forward enough but we would have to make sure that we both pictured the same bike in our minds that we would send to Johnny by thought. So a week before Johnny's birthday Clive and I walked into the local bicycle shop to look at "Chopper" bikes.

The shopkeeper approached us and the conversation went something along these lines.

"Good afternoon gentlemen, can I help you?"

"Yes, we are looking for a Chopper bicycle for a five-year- old"

"Oh, good, we have a large selection here of the most popular models. May I ask is the bike for a boy or a girl".

"Boy".

"Is he a big five or a small five".

"Big five".

"I see, well these here start from £75 and go through to about £200. We do keep a large selection of spares and accessories..."

At this point I had to leave Clive and the shopkeeper to it because I began to have a fit of the giggles. After all if the shopkeeper knew that we had come to look at bicycles for a "dead" boy to whom we were going to send a bike in thought, I am sure he would have sent for the ambulance to take us back to the asylum.

Well the 15th November arrived and Clive and I sat in our circle. No sooner had we started and Johnny was through, very very exited.

"I've been, I've been, I've been!" he said.

"Where have you been" I asked.

"I've been and got my bike! I can't ride it yet, I will have to get the seat lowered. Its got a bell and a toot toot (horn). It's my birthday and I'm five!" Johnny was so excited he could hardly talk and needless to say did not stay very long. He had to show all his Spirit friends his new shinning bicycle.

It was not long before Johnny learned to ride his bike. He said it was not difficult to learn really and being a Spirit boy when he fell off he did not hurt himself because he did not have a physical body.

Now Johnny can quiet often been seen pedalling up and down the aisles of the various churches we attended. Sometimes he will pedal right across the platform, but schh do not let on, as some of our crusty Spiritualists might not approve.

Johnny and I have great fun together and he is with me nearly all the time. He comes with me to the office, churches, holidays and whenever I need a parking space I just have to ask Johnny a few minutes before we are due to arrive and there is always one available. Johnny has decided to stay at five as it is the age he feels most comfortable with and thinks that "grown ups" have lots of problems to deal with.

There are lots of little stories about Johnny and the things he has been upto since we met but perhaps we can share some of these another time. Till then Best Wishes from us both."

I am sure you will agree that this is a very sad tale but with a happy ending. Indeed Johnny has proved to be, for me, one of my spiritual highlights for a very special experience which I was totally unprepared for. I had never seen spirit and was always, to be honest, a bit envious of those that could because it must be a truly remarkable experience.

In my job I did a lot of driving and would spend this time thinking and strategising on various deals that I had going on at the time. I would have a pad and pen on the passenger seat next to me and once I had, what I felt was a good thought, I would jot it down. This was a bit dangerous at times as I often just continued to drive at the same time as writing.

So it occurred to me that it would be far better and a safer to have one of these small portable micro cassette recorders and just speak into it when I had a brainwave. So on Saturday 29th July 1982 just after 9.00am with the street almost deserted I was walking along Station Road in Harrow. There were two shops that caught my eye which were almost opposite each other, Currys and Dixons.

I walked into Currys which was empty apart from the store staff and walked over to the area where they had electrical gadgets. As I made my way to this counter I caught a glimpse, out the corner of my eye, of a small boy sitting on the floor watching the cartoons on the shop TVs. I momentarily stopped in my tracks and did a double take because this little boy looked just like I pictured Johnny in my mind's eye. The likeness was uncanny. Nobody was taking any attention of this little boy and indeed I looked around the shop to see if I could see his parents. I could not and thought that perhaps they were huddled around a tall fridge freezer or something.

I looked at a few recorders but this little boy kept playing on my mind and I turned round to look again. He was still sitting on the floor watching cartoons. Again I looked up and down the store for his parents but could not see any. He just looks like Johnny I said to myself.

I left the store and crossed over the road to Dixons to have a look at their recorders but my mind was still back in Currys and this little boy. So I quickly left Dixons and went back to Currys but this little boy was not there now. I went outside and looked up and down the road but did not see anything. I was truly mystified. I went back into Currys and bought a Sony M9 Cassette Recorder for £34.99 and some batteries for 79p. I still have the receipt.

This experience played on my mind continually because the little boy was just like Johnny. A few days later Clive was doing a group sitting and Woo Wang spoke to everyone individually. At the end of the evening he turns to me, as was his usual custom, and we would exchange a few words. I ask him about this little boy in the shop and Woo Wang chuckled. I said he looked just like Johnny.

Woo Wang then explained that the little boy was indeed Johnny and he was there just for me. I asked for clarification, what did he mean by "just for me." Woo Wang explained that Johnny wanted very much for his daddy to be able to see him so he asked spirit to help and send all the power and energy, so that I would see him in the physical form. I asked Woo Wang to clarify what this actually meant and he told me that it was only me who could see Johnny and not the other people in the store. That made sense because nobody else took any notice of him.

Then I asked if I had gone upto Johnny and given him a cuddle would I have physically felt him or would I in effect be cuddling thin air. Woo Wang said that I would have felt Johnny just the same as if I had been cuddling anybody else. OK, but what would the others in the store see if I did this and Woo Wang explained that they would just see me putting my arms around thin air.

I was quiet astonished with what I had been told on a number of different levels. Firstly that I had in fact seen spirit and in exactly the same way as I see anybody else and secondly that I had not taken this rare opportunity to go up to Johnny and give him a cuddle which I have always wanted to do. But I still puzzle over what actually goes on in the brain (if that is the right place) that enabled me to see Johnny and others not.

Since that day back in 1982 I have never see Johnny again, although I do feel his presence around me continually. Perhaps one day I will again see him as clearly as then and this time, hopefully, I won't fluff the opportunity to give him a long cuddle.

A few years ago we bought an African Grey Parrott who is called "Geordie" (he originally came from Newcastle). He is very a talkative bird and says the usual things that we have taught him like, "Good morning, going shopping, Geordie made a mess, cup of tea, sandwiches etc". However just recently when I was working in the kitchen Geordie was talking away to himself when to my astonishment he said "my name's Johnny" and then a little later "hello Johnny". Now nobody has taught him to say this and he could not have picked it up from us as it is not something we say.

But I do know that Johnny is around all the time and I can only conclude that he has picked it up from him. But how is it possible for a spirit boy without a physical body to speak to a parrot? I can only conclude that Geordie picks this up psychically from Johnny.

Other spirit children in our lives include Richard who is quiet a handful and very mischievous. I wrote an article about him which was published in 1993 and is at the Appendix. It will give you a good idea what we have to put up with. Quiet a few people have heard Richard and Johnny speak in the churches because, as mentioned earlier, when Clive does a trance questions and answers with Woo Wang, these two quiet often come in at the end have the audience in stitches with their comments.

In addition around us we have Brenda who is Richards girlfriend. Her last incarnation was as a maid in a large house in Bedford. Richard tells us in his own inimitable way that "Bren is lovely girl and has got a good pair of headlamps".

Michael has been with us since the late 90s and is a downes syndrome child of 14. He was taken to a children's home run by some nuns who were not of the most spiritual and loving nature and it was a place he did not enjoy. He was taken there by his father who could not take the stigma of having a downes syndrome child. His mother on the other hand wanted Michael to stay at home but lost out to his domineering father.

Michael continues to grow in the world of spirit.

The final three in our little family are Tommy who originally lived out in India and returned to the UK after his parents were killed. Jenny who is about 3 and loves to dance and baby Paul. We do not know anything about their backgrounds.

Some of these children have decided to remain at the age they were when we first met them while other have chosen to continue and grow in the world of spirit. It is their free will.

Although these are all spirit children they do behave just like ordinary physical children. A typical example of this is at Christmas time when we quiet often find presents under the tree have been shuffled about and come into the lounge and some of the decorations on the tree are still swinging about. Christmas In our home is a very special and magical time full of much emotion, excitement and love.

15

EXPLANATIONS

This chapter is to show and explain all the different events that happened to both of us and how our lives have weaved in and out over many years not only in this life but also previous incarnations.

Woo Wang is very critical and instrumental in much that has happened in our lives, not because he has told us what to do or what will happen, but because he has been our inspiration in many of the things that we have done and achieved. He has really been watching over us as we have gone through this life. It has also been him who has explained so many things, which now that we know, helps us to understand our pathway as well.

In order to help with these "explanations" it would be helpful to go back to a time even before Clive's birth. Our view on life and evolvement is that in the world of spirit that are many different pools of spirit each with similarly evolved spiritual beings. Each one of these pools is striving to become more spiritual and this can be achieved by either reincarnating to the earth plane (and learning more lessons) or continuing ones evolvement in the world of spirit.

Woo Wang has told us that Clive and I come from one particular pool of spirit. In the spirit world there are many different pools of spirit each with like minded or evolved spirits. Clive's spirit self had already completed all of its reincarnations to the earth plane and could have continued progressing in the spirit world. However my spirit had not.

My spirit therefore decide that it should return, once more, to the earth plane to learn some final lessons before continuing development in the spirit world. But my spirit did not want to come back on its own and therefore persuaded the spirit of Clive to reincarnate with me. We therefore chose a mother (Bertha Daniels) and she was having twins, us. At the time of birth the spirit of Clive was born first but my spirit had second thoughts and returned back to the world of spirit immediately on birth. Hence the second twin was still-born. This experience explains why Clive as a child never felt complete and was always in effect looking for his missing brother/spiritual partner.

So my spirit has decided to go back to the world of spirit and leave Clive on his own. Not a nice thing to do as I am sure you would agree. But some years later my spirit does indeed reincarnate when Wojtek is born. So we now have both spirits in the physical form. That is to say Clive who lives in Litherland near Liverpool and me in London.

The first time we meet in the physical sense is in 1976 at Rayners Lane Spiritualist Church and as I mentioned earlier there was "something" about Clive which I could not pinpoint and he too had similar thoughts about me. Now that we know we both came from the same pool of spirit things start to make sense.

Things also made a lot more sense after I had a trance session with Woo Wang on a one to one basis where he told me of a number of my previous incarnations and how my spirit and the spirit of Clive had been joined together many times before. Sometimes as a couple and sometimes in the male or female form. It was at one of these sessions that Woo Wang told me that in our last life, which was in Victorian times, we again were together.

The spirit of Clive was in a female form and born in England while I was male but originally from Belgium. We lived together although we were not married. Our work was that of going to music halls where I would play the piano and my partner (Clive) would sing. We lived in rented rooms and times were hard to the extent that we, on several occasions, did a "moonlight flight" to avoid paying the long outstanding rent. We had a daughter and her name was Lydia. She passed into the world of spirit at age twelve and a half with diphtheria. Yes that's right, the very same spirit girl who now works with Clive and first made herself know to him when he too had a sore throat.

The chandelier that has been mentioned earlier was a made up piece which utilised various crystal droplets from a number of separate units. But several droplets are the same droplets that were in a house where Lydia lived while on the earth plane in Victorian times. Indeed even today when ever Clive cleans it he can hear Lydia giggling in the background.

So the fact that we are together and get on very well is really no real surprise and was really inevitable because wherever our respective free-will took us we would surely, once again, meet.

16

SPIRITUAL ANECDOTES

As we have jointly been working for spirit for over 80 years we have naturally many experiences that we can call upon. Some are funny some are sad but all have moulded us on the journey we have taken. Below are just a few examples.

Joe Benjamin
Some of you may know of a medium by the name of Joe Benjamin. He was the first medium to give a very significant and accurate message to Clive the like of which has never been repeated to this day. In the early 1950s Joe would hold meetings at the Alliance Hall in Victoria, London. These meeting would always be packed out and many could not, as a result, even get into the building.

When Clive was 17 he took his driving test and passed. That same evening he went to the London Spiritual Mission, Pembridge Place, London for their midweek service. He sat on the back row in between two people. The medium that night was Joe Benjamin. When Joe started to demonstrate he said that he had a young lady from Liverpool with him who was holding a baby in her arms and she was looking for her son. Nobody would accept this information and although Clive could understand it he remained silent.

The service continued and other messages were given and accepted and then it came to the end of the service and the chairman called Joe to time. But he said that he could not stop yet as this young Liverpool lady with the baby in her arms was still present.

Joe then said that he wanted to go to the back of the church and said that there was a man with a beard, next to him he could not see because the person in the row in front was large and then there was a lady. He said that he wanted to speak to the person sitting in between them. That was Clive. He said to Clive "why is this lady talking about Liverpool?" Clive said "I am from Liverpool." Joe then went on to give Clive very specific information some of which he did not even know about and had to check with his family. All of it proved to be totally correct.

Medium caught short
I have mentioned earlier about Rayners Lane Spiritualist Church which was situated under a parade of shops in a garage. This little church did not have a toilet and all visiting mediums were reminded to use the facilities at Rayners Lane Station before serving the church.

Well one particular Sunday night the visiting medium was a rather elderly and portly lady with a good stubble around her chin. She went up onto the raised platform and sat down in the mediums chair with her legs parted in a most unwise fashion. The service duly started and she had already given her address and was sitting down before the next hymn which preceded the clairvoyance. During the singing of this hymn the chairman was shocked and horrified to see a pool of urine running down the back of the mediums chair, dripping onto the linoleum of the rostrum and then trickling to the front of the rostrum and down onto the carpet below. All in full view of the congregation.

The medium was completely oblivious to what was happening and just kept smiling to the congregation as they looked back aghast and in bewilderment. She demonstrated clairvoyance and after the service as she left the rostrum in a very wet skirt she insisted in kissing members of the congregation as she made her way back to the mediums room.

Even after vigorous cleaning the stain on the lino could not be removed and it stayed there for many years till the rostrum was carpeted.

Healer Smashed
At this particular time there was Deep Trance Healer who advertised in the psychic press and was visiting churches to demonstrate his "gift". We decided to go and see him at work and arrived at the church in London. The room where the meeting was to be held had a stage on which was a large chair and a small round table with a picture of the healer's healing guide who was a North American Indian.

The healer came on stage and explained that he was going to go into a very deep trance to perform his healing and that this was quiet unusual to do etc. Patients were informed to come onto the stage and sit on a chair and he would then perform deep trance healing.

The evening started and the healer stood behind his healing chair and held onto the top of it and contorted his face in many different directions for a minute or so. He was now in deep trance "apparently". He nodded his head which was a signal for the first patient to come forward and be seated in the healing chair.

This they did and the medium, still contorting

116

his face with his eyes closed, started the laying on of hands. Unfortunately as he moved around the patient he bumped into the small table and the picture of his guide toppled over and fell to the ground with a loud crash as the glass shattered. The healer, remember he is supposed to be in deep trance, opened his eyes immediately and looked down on the floor at the shattered picture of his guide and said "oh bloody hell!" he then picked up the picture, placed it back on the table and again immediately went back to his deep trance state.

Flight of fancy

Clive was running a development circle at the church which met every Monday evening. There was a lady there who was very keen to develop her psychic gifts and would pray most earnestly that this would happen and soon.

After a few weeks of attending the circle she came bouncing into the church full of excitement and rushed over to Clive and said, "it's started to happen, it's started to happen!" When Clive asked "what do you mean?" she explained that she had started to hear spirit voices at home. Clive said that was great but what is it that they are saying. She said she could not quiet make it out it seemed like they were saying "ooo ooo, ooo ooo." Clive told her not to worry because over time she may be able to hear more clearly.

The next week again she bounces in more excited saying that it is still happening but on questioning it was no different from the previous week. The following week the same thing happens again but this time she says to Clive that he must come home with her and listen for himself. Now Clive was a young man in his 30s and this was a divorcee in her 40s.

Clive did go home with her and told her to do exactly the same things that she normally does and then they would see what happens. It was then that she told him that the noises are only heard in her bedroom. So up to the bedroom they go. A cautious Clive tells her to do what she normally does and she knelt down by her bed and started praying. Sure enough the noises started again "ooo   ooo, ooo   ooo." "There" she said to Clive, "can you hear them?" "Yes," said Clive, "it's obvious you have got pigeons in the loft"

Not your fault
We had arrived to carry out a Sunday evening service and had just been seated ready for the service to commence. While the chairman was doing the usual introductions Clive and I looked around the congregation and we both noticed a man who had a tremendous air of sadness around him. He looked very gloomy, depressed and sad.

It came to the clairvoyant part of the service and time was getting on. The next message was to be the last of the night and Clive was drawn to this very same man. He told him various things which he could understand but then he came to what was to be the key part of the message. He told him that he had a young girl with him, a teenager, and that she had come back specifically to forgive him and also to stress that it was not his fault. She was most insistent on this point. The man understood this and sat in a stunned daze.

The service ended and we all went for a cup of tea and mingled with the congregation. The man came upto Clive still in quiet an emotional state and thanked him very much for his message. He went on to explain that a few months earlier while driving home at night

118

he had run over and killed a teenage girl and although the police had cleared him of any blame he still felt very responsible. But the message from Clive had lifted a great weight from him and you could see the complete change in this man's demeanour as a result. He left the church a very different person.

Don't understand a thing

Clive was demonstrating clairvoyance at a church (remember the medium's job is to prove survival). Sitting in the front row with her arms folded sat a middle-aged lady who had a "I dare you to give me a message" look about her. Clive hoped he would not have to go to her but as it turned out Lydia stood behind this lady and pointed at her.

Clive started to give her various people and explained what they passed with and how they looked while on the earth plane etc. But to everything he said she just barked back "No!" Clive persevered but all to no avail, she just came back with the same retort. So eventually Clive said to her, "Do you not understand any of the people that I am bringing to you?". She replied "Oh yes, I know them all, but they are all dead".

Timely confusion

I have already mentioned various spirits that have spoken through Clive that need to be rescued. But other spirits have spoken too and here is just an example of how confusing things can get when there is a 150 years or so difference between lifetimes.

I was having a one to one session with Woo Wang one evening when he told me that a new healing guide (a North American Indian) had linked with me and that if I wanted he would allow him to come through and speak to me. I readily agreed and sat back and waited with eager anticipation. Shortly afterwards I was greeted by a deep voice and the new guide introduced himself as Strong Horse. We started having a general chat and then he asked me if I lived in a Tipi. At the time I was living in Harrow in my first floor flat so I said no I lived in a flat. With that he held out his arm at right angles to his body and made a wide sweep from left to right. He was obviously confused because there were no such things as flats in his day and the only flat he could relate to was the flat of the land.

So I thought that I would be clever and asked him if he understood what a cabin was. He said he did. So I said that I live in a cabin on top of another cabin. He was very puzzled by this as it clearly made no sense at all to him. Next he asked me if I had a horse. I said no but I have a motor car. As soon as I said motor car I knew I had lost him so I asked him if he understood a stagecoach. He said he did, so I said I had a stagecoach but with no horses. Again he looked puzzled and asked me "how it go place to place without horses." I then went on to explain about an engine but again I lost him.

Although this is amusing, if you think about it, but why should someone from his time on the earth plane automatically know anything about current times.

Knickers?
One evening we were booked to do a trance group. I always explained at the time of the booking that the key purpose of the evening is to prove survival and that it is definitely not a fortune telling session. We arrived at the house and were met by a lady who took us into the lounge were there were six other ladies. They all looked what I can only describe as a bit "shifty".

120

The evening started and all went well and we finished and were having a cup of tea with everyone, when the door-bell rang. One of the women looked out through the closed curtains and then flew into a mad panic. Her husband had come to collect her but not only had he arrived early he had also come with some of the other women's husbands too.

The host oblivious to any panic just opened the door and showed them into the hall. From there they could see both Clive and I sitting in the lounge and they looked at us in quiet a mystified way. One of the women seeing this quickly slammed the door.

We learnt later that several of the women had told their husbands that they had gone to a Lingerie Party

Message changed my life
From time to time the messages that Clive has given have proved to have had a very dramatic effect on the lives of the people that he has spoken to. Quiet a number of times someone has come upto him and thanked him most earnestly for the message that he has given, sometimes years earlier. They have told him that as a result of what he told them he has changed their lives for the better. These are truly humbling experiences which particularly at times when you yourself may feel a bit down bring you right back and confirm to you that doing this work for spirit is correct.

Family affairs
Some years ago a young man in his early 30s came for a sitting with Clive. The sitting went very well except for one area which had the young man baffled. Clive told the young man that he had a gentleman in the world of spirit who wanted to make contact with him.

The gentleman told him that he was his father and had passed into the world of spirit with a cancer condition.

The young man said he could not understand this at all as his father was still very much alive and he had just left him at home watching television. Clive continued with more information about this gentleman describing him in some detail. The gentleman was most insistent that he was the young man's father. This was all to no avail as the young man could just not accept this part of the sitting. All the other bits of information in the sitting he could understand totally.

The young man left and Clive was concerned at this one aspect of the message. Why was this not understood.

Now we both knew the mother of this young man who had told us that she had been "quite a girl" in her time. The day after the sitting she phoned up Clive in a most anxious and worried state. She told Clive that her son had mentioned to her the one aspect of the sitting that he could not understand and quizzed Clive on what he had said.

The reason for this "confusion" was that she had had an affair many years ago and her son was the result. The father of the boy was in fact the man Clive had described in detail who had passed into spirit with cancer many years ago. Neither her current husband or son knew anything about the affair.

17

FREEWILL

In my many discussions with Clive over the years this topic has come up. Clive has said that he never had any freewill because if he did he would certainly not have chosen to give up his free time to serve churches and meetings over the last 50 years or so. Instead he would have devoted his time to breeding his dogs and having a great social life. But there has always been a part of him that has wanted to serve.

So he was being pulled in two different directions. This is really quiet easy to explain because his "spirit self" that is to say the spirit within the physical body wanted to work for spirit. However his physical self wanted to do other things which were on the material level (i.e. his dog breeding and socialising). We are after all a spiritual being but housed in a physical body.

So as with everything in life you have to find a "balance" in the things that you do. If you do to much of one thing then something else will suffer. When you have found this "balance" then in my experience you find people who are settled and contented in their life.

One example of being out of balance is shown in an event which happened over 40 years ago. It was when Clive was running a circle and one of the sitters was a gentleman who was interested in Spiritualism but was a bit uneasy about it. In the circle room, which was at the top of the house, was a dachshund dog. This dog had a paralysed back and was unable to walk. When Clive took her out he had to place a towel under her hind quarters to enable her to do her toilet. He had taken her to the vet who had said that the best thing to do was to have her put down as she would not recover. Clive asked the vet if she was in any pain and the vet replied that she could not feel a thing. As this was the case Clive said he would take her home for a little while longer.

During the circle this particular night Clive had allowed Woo Wang to come through and speak to the sitters. At the end of the evening before he left Woo Wang spoke to the gentleman mentioned earlier and told him to give the dog spiritual healing after the circle finished.

The circle finished and everyone but the gentleman walked down two flights of stairs to the kitchen for a cup of tea, chat and a cigarette. During this time the gentleman was giving the dog healing upstairs. After about 10 minutes the gentleman joined everyone in the kitchen.

Some minutes later while everyone was still chatting and smoking they heard a scratching at the kitchen door. Clive went over to the door, opened it and there stood his "paralysed" dachshund wagging her tail. She had just walked down two flights stairs! Everyone was shocked, the gentleman who had given her healing a few moments earlier was more shocked than most. Not only shocked but he was also frightened by what had happened and the "power" that he had. The dog lived for quiet a few years without any reoccurrence of the paralysis.

This healing was one of those events where there are immediate results. However since that day the gentleman has not done any healing because he was frightened by this experience. What a terrible shame as here was someone who could of done so much for those in need but decided against it.

So this is an example of the physical/material freewill having the majority say, while his spirit self was screaming out to do more. The net result for this gentleman is that there has been a massive imbalance with his spiritual and material life. He has remained unfulfilled in this life and has had spent a very unsettled life full of anger and made life unpleasant for those closest to him.

But having said that this feeling of being unfulfilled may well be the very experience that he has come back to the earth plane to go through.

So I feel our journey in this particular life is already set but how we get from point "A" to point "B" is our freewill.

18

THE WORK GOES ON

Now our working schedule is not as ferocious as before as we have to take account of age (Clive is in his 70s now). We have both found it difficult, at times, to strike a happy balance between our spiritual work, material work and private lives. More often than not the spiritual work won at the expense of our free time. This was because when I received the phone call to serve I found it difficult to say no because always at the back of my mind was the possibility that at that particular service there could be someone in desperate need and they might find comfort either from a spirit message or just by being there.

Some of you might feel that the various difficulties that Clive has experienced in his lifetime have effected him in a detrimental way. I feel that this is not so as it is because of these experiences he has become a stronger person and at the same time can empathise more with those that he speaks to at the churches.

Today there is a big difference in spiritualism because since the late 1990s there has been a great upsurge in psychic phenomenon awareness, as a result of TV and theatre shows, often at the expense and indeed detriment of true spiritualism. Indeed, even those that now run many spiritualist churches, are unaware of the difference between spiritualism and psychism.

When Clive started his spiritual work over 50 years ago he made a bargain with spirit. That was if they kept him fit and well then he in turn would work for them. Over the years Clive has never let a church down as a result of ill-health. Indeed he could be feeling dreadful with flu but as soon as he got to the church his condition never effected him and he worked perfectly well.

I did an exercise where I looked at the numbers of appointments Clive carried out per week over the years he has worked and the average number of messages he typically gives each time. To date and to our amazement he has given over 40,000 messages!

We will continue to serve spirit and take appointments as long as we are asked to and are healthy enough to do so, and Clive and I will, as ever, stay spiritually entwined.

APPENDIX

This article was first published in a monthly magazine journal for spiritualists called the *Here and There* in 1993.

RICHARD'S JOURNEY

This is a true story which encompasses a whole range of emotions ranging from great joy to great sadness. Let me introduce you to Richard first of all as he is the star and without whom the journey would not have taken place.

Richard was born on 13th September 1926 in Bermondsey, East London. His family background is not totally clear, however we do know that he had an elder half brother David. His brother was the son of his legal father although Richard's father was one of his mothers "man friends".

When the Second World War started both Richard and David were evacuated to Wales where they spent some time working for a lady, with some other children, on some kind of smallholding. When Richard was fourteen it was decided that he should return to London with his brother and be sent to work in a munitions factory. It was while Richard and David were travelling back on the train to London that they encountered a German air raid. The train was bombed and they were both killed outright.

We now come to 1981 and a circle held in Harrow, Middlesex. The two sitters were Clive Daniels and myself. Over a period of several months while in quiet meditation various Spirits would take control of Clive, some would speak readily others would not. On this particular occasion I was aware that someone had taken control of Clive and seemed to be mumbling away to themselves. I listened intently, but all I heard was a begrudging voice saying, "I've done it! I've done it!" Done what I thought. So I asked, "What have you done?" The terse response was "I've cut the toilet paper!" What a strange reply I thought, perhaps someone a bit mentally unstable was through. What should I do? Treat them normally I thought and introduce yourself to them. "Hello my name is Wojtek, what's yours?" I asked. "I'm telling you nofink!" came the reply. "Can't you tell me your name" I said. "Yours ain't a English name is it?" came the reply. "That's right, it's a Polish name...! I was interrupted. "Is that near Germany?" he asked. "Yes, it's next door to Germany," I answered. He shouted back at me "I'm tellin you nofink. We've been told about people like you. You're a spy and I aint tellin you nofink!"

Well to cut a long story short this Spirit was that of David. He had not realised that he had passed into the world of Spirit although did know that "something" had happened on the train. After quiet a long discussion I managed to convince him that he was still very much alive but just in a different way. He explained his reluctance to speak to me was because he had been told not to speak to strangers as they might be spies.

Before David left I asked him why at the beginning

he had said that he had "cut the toilet paper". David explained that the lady they were staying with allocated jobs to them all and his was to cut the newspaper into squares for "the lavvy".

During the next few weeks David would come and speak through Clive in the circle. He told me about his brother Richard who was still very frightened and was hiding in a hole and would not come out. So we set about encouraging Richard to leave the hole and come out into the light. David would talk to him and also bring other Spirit people to visit while Clive and I would send out our thoughts. After some weeks a shy and a little withdrawn but abrasive Richard emerged. Since that time David has taken a very low profile in our lives and Richard has done the complete opposite.

Richard would come through in the circle from time to time and we would have a chat about all sorts of things. It also took him some time to believe that I indeed was not a spy but just had a Polish name. Richard is around us all the time now and can be quiet a little mischief. He was a little clumsy in his ways and would often refer to himself as being "daft". He had a habit of screwing up his eyes, could read little and would hear what and when he wanted to. It was only after several months that Clive and I realised that perhaps the reason he is clumsy is because he cannot see clearly. So in our thoughts we set about getting his eyes tested and now Richard has his glasses and can see very well. Truth is that he does not need glasses but wears them when he wants to look serious, because when in Spirit if you want good eyesight then you can have it. Richard did not realise this until it was explained to him.

A few years have passed and Clive and I were invited to go and work in Germany for a week and carry out some public demonstrations of clairvoyance, healing and a seminar. We accepted and on the appointed day set out for the airport together with our Spirit friends. These of course included Richard who was a little reluctant to go because of his war memories even though we had told him that the war had been over for many years.

Now I am not blaming Richard for what happened next but... We arrived at the airport and boarded the plane and waited, and waited, and waited. Eventually the pilot spoke and apologised for the delay informing us that they were experiencing some "technical difficulties". We waited another half hour or so and were then told that we would have to change planes as the technical fault could not be cleared. We changed planes and eventually arrived in Germany. The following year when we went again, we left home in heaps of time only to experience one of the worst traffic jams on the M1. We had to detour off the motorway and only made it to the airport with seconds to spare. Richard kept a very low profile in Germany. He told us he had to make notes to give to Mr. Churchill when he got back.

Now we come to the main part of Richard's journey. In October 1990 I visited Poland to attend a family wedding. As usual my car had a number of Spirit passengers including Richard. The wedding was a great success and much fun and happiness was had. The following day I visited a number of towns with my mother to see old friends and places. A few days later I was back in England.

Now it is the first Friday after I returned and circle night. Richard came through and told us what he had been upto while in Poland. Richard had met another Spirit of a man who asked whether Richard wanted to go and visit Auschwitz. Richard agreed to go. When he got there he was confronted by the horror and sadness of that place. There were still many Spirits there who had not left the camp and progressed. Whether it was because they did not know they could progress away or because they were still searching for their loved ones, I do not know. The sight upset Richard and saddened him a great deal, but he wanted to help. He spoke to two Jewish boys of about the same age as himself and explained to them that they could leave this place if they wanted to. They were now free. The Jewish boys did not believe Richard and told him to go away. Richard persisted, much to their annoyance, so much so that they threatened to chase him and punch him. Undaunted, Richard carried on and indeed they did chase him, but when they were clear of the camp Richard stopped, turned around and showed them that they had left the camp behind. He continued to explain about the Spirit world and slowly managed to get their confidence. So much so that he brought them back to England with him so that they could rest, be fed and clothed before progressing further. Richard also explained that his two Jewish friends were however very worried because they did have parents and sisters who were still held at the camp and they wanted so much to bring them out too. Richard therefore decided to go back with them and search the camp for their families.

They were away for almost a week and their presence was missed. Clive and I were beginning to get a little concerned, wondering how everything was progressing and whether they had been successful in their search. But there was no need to worry because shortly afterwards there was much commotion as everybody returned back safe and reunited. One of the Jewish boys found both his parents and two sisters, the other both his parents and one sister. So we now had nine visitors with us.

We were very much aware of their presence in the house and the fear and uncertainty that was with them. They would hide any food that was given to them and tuck it away into their meagre possessions. They were very uncertain of Clive and myself and their new surroundings and took time to realise that they were still alive and had left Auschwitz behind. We were also very aware of their worship and singing as they gave thanks for their reunion. They all stayed with us for several weeks before they moved onto their new spiritual home where hopefully they will be able to progress on their Spiritual pathway.

Since that time Richard has made further journeys to Auschwitz with the two Jewish boys and have brought out more people. Now the two Jewish boys are making the journeys on their own and more and more people are being brought out.

Richard's life has developed further as he now accompanies me to the office and is very much around helping me in the job that I do. I call him my "right hand man" and am aware of his presence and suggestions to me that do help very much. Now I would be at a real loss if he decided that he wanted to progress away from me. He calls me his dad and is pleased with his new life now as it is the first time he has been appreciated and understood by those around him. He can be a bit "trying" at times but I would not change him for the world. He has taught me a lot and am sure will continue to do so. I hope that I in turn can do justice to him.

Keep up the good work Richard.